Protectionism or Liberalism in International Economic Relations?

Schriften zu Regional- und Verkehrsproblemen
in Industrie- und Entwicklungsländern
Herausgegeben von J. Heinz Müller und Theodor Dams

Band 50

Protectionism or Liberalism in International Economic Relations?

Current Issues in Japan and Germany

edited by

Theodor Dams

Takashi Matsugi

Duncker & Humblot · Berlin

CIP-Titelaufnahme der Deutschen Bibliothek

Protectionism or Liberalism in International Economic Relations?:
Current Issues in Japan and Germany / ed. by Theodor Dams;
Takashi Matsugi. – Berlin: Duncker und Humblot, 1991
(Schriften zu Regional- und Verkehrsproblemen in Industrie- und Entwicklungsländern; Bd. 50)
ISBN 3-428-07105-0
NE: Dams, Theodor [Hrsg.]; GT

Fotoprint: Werner Hildebrand, Berlin 65
Printed in Germany

ISSN 0582-0170
ISBN 3-428-07105-0

Editors' Foreword

This volume contains the proceedings of the 11th Joint Seminar of the Faculties of Economics of Nagoya and Freiburg Universities, held in Nagoya in March 1988. The series of Joint Seminars is concerned with topical economic issues and with the Japanese and German economies in particular.

The current volume covers the question of the foreign trade strategy in leading developed economies. Since the late 1970s, tendencies towards a so-called "new protectionism" have been noted throughout the world. However, economists have not tired to argue in favor of free trade.

Obviously, the debate on "liberalism or protectionism" is a complex one, with different views to be taken into account. Therefore, it was considered an adequate subject for a Nagoya-Freiburg-Seminar. Management scientists, economic theoricians, specialists of economic policy and public finance treat the issues from different angles. Special emphasis was laid on covering the intricacies of the Japanese and German economies. This holds for a discussion of small- and medium-sized enterprises in Japan or German assistance schemes for the setting-up of businesses, for instance. It is hoped that by covering a wide range of topics, this book can contribute to a more balanced view of an "eternal" economic problem.

Publication of these proceedings was made possible through the financial assistance from the Wissenschaftliche Gesellschaft Freiburg im Breisgau. Editorial work was carried out in the Institute of Development Policy of Freiburg University, coordinated by Dr. Werner Pascha, type-set by Hans Köhne. The cooperation of the Nagoya working group under its chairman, Professor Takashi Matsugi, is also gratefully acknowledged.

Freiburg, October 1990

J. Heinz Müller *Theodor Dams*

Table of Contents

Is there a Macroeconomic Case for Protection?

Oliver Landmann[1]

1. Introduction: The rise of protectionism

There can be no doubt: Protectionism is riding high again. Gone are the golden 1950s and 1960s when the trade barriers of the interwar period were torn down in a determined effort to liberalize economic relations among industrial nations. To be sure, even in that heyday of trade liberalization, there were pressures working toward increased protection. But they were weak and swamped by the impact of a number of countervailing forces which included the still fresh memory of the disastrous experience of the 1930s, strong U.S. leadership in the liberalization process, increasingly efficient means of transportation and communication, and perhaps most importantly, a background of rapid and steady economic growth[2].

The momentum of trade liberalization began to slow down in the 1970s as latent structural problems in many industrial countries became more pronounced due to the well known macroeconomic shocks of that decade. Even then, however, much of the protectionism - not all, but much - was confined to rhetoric rather than action. World trade continued to outpace the growth of world GNP, with increasingly outward-oriented developing countries appropriating an ever larger share of that trade.

Protectionist pressures intensified in the 1980s when the world economy was struck by another severe recession and the outbreak of the LDC debt crisis. The strain showed most in the United States whose balance of trade moved into deficit on an unprecedented scale.

---

1) Valuable comments from Martin *Bronfenbrenner* and the participants of the 1988 Nagoya-Freiburg Seminar are gratefully acknowledged.

2) For an instructive review of the rise and eventual reversal of trade liberalization in the postwar period, see *Krueger* 1988.

U.S. manufacturing industries were especially hard hit by the desperate attempt of Latin American debtors to turn around their net export position and, of course, by the real appreciation of the U.S. dollar. Calls for protection grew louder and resulted in a number of import restraining measures in sensitive sectors. Even though the *Reagan* administration was ideologically more committed to free trade than most of its predecessors, it was not able to provide strong leadership in promoting the liberalization of world trade. Instead, it felt forced to make repeated protectionist concessions just to keep the pressure from getting even worse.

The spreading protectionism did not roll back the achievements reached within the framework of GATT. Tariffs continued to fall. Among developed countries they averaged little more than 5 % on industrial products after completion of the Tokyo round (see Figure 1). However, there was an explosive increase in the number of non-tariff trade barriers such as quotas, voluntary export restraints, idiosyncratic national standards and other forms of 'managed trade'. As far as the industrial countries are concerned, Figure 1 shows that the non-tariff barriers are heavily concentrated on aging industries - steel, vehicles and textiles, in particular. These are exactly the industries in which the highly developed economies are gradually losing their comparative advantage vis-a-vis developing and newly industrialized countries.

This is in line with the observation that the growing impediments to free trade were rarely part of any comprehensive macroeconomic strategy, but rather case-by-case emergency measures to save sensitive sectors from painful adjustments or at least to slow down the displaçement of jobs. This is not to deny, of course, that a deteriorating macroeconomic environment greatly strengthened the forces opposing structural change. But only in exceptional circumstances, protectionist measures were taken explicitly to address a macroeconomic problem rather than a sectorial problem; and then the problem was likely to be a balance-of-payments emergency as in the case of *Nixon*'s 1971 import surcharge.

Today, however, protectionism is again very much present in the macroeconomic policy debate, especially in the United States. This is perhaps not surprising in view of the huge and persistent U.S. trade deficit and the general consensus on the need to do something about it. Not only politicians, but even respected U.S. economists have publicly advocated the use of protectionist policies to facilitate the

Figure 1 : More Barriers Block Trade while Tariffs have Tumbled

Number of restraint arrangements on manufactured exports

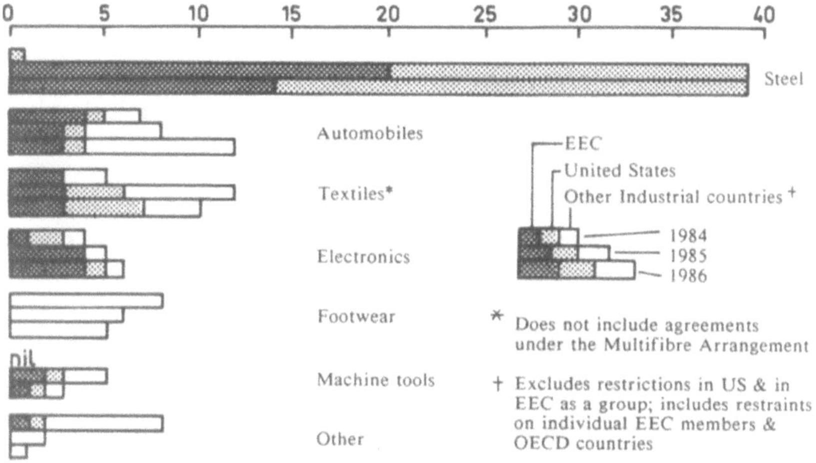

Average tariffs for industrial products

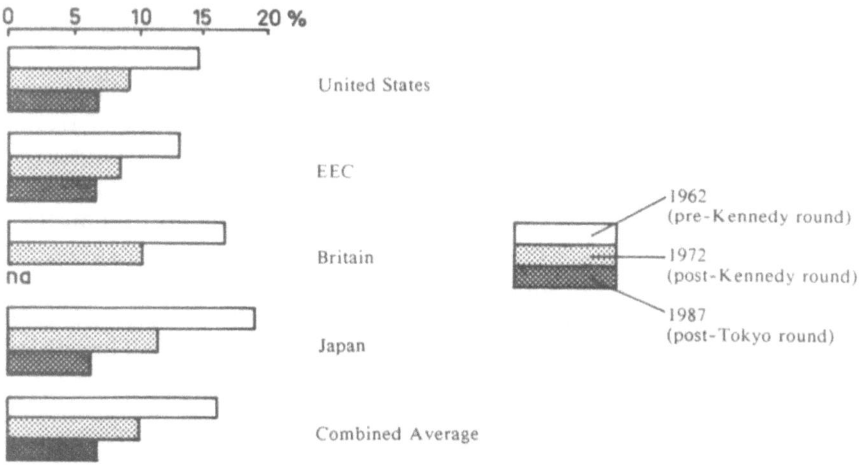

Source: The Economist, 20 February 1988; based on GATT data

adjustment. The case for protectionism appears all the more persuasive as almost three years of pronounced currency depreciation have failed to leave any noticeable mark in the trade figures - at least up to the final quarter of 1987[3].

The general line of argument underlying the current protectionist sentiment in the United States can be inferred from the following propositions, all quoted from *Culbertson* (1987):

- "The free trade theory is false. It is not true that unregulated foreign trade is automatically beneficial to both nations involved in a trading arrangement".

- "To be beneficial to both countries, trade, except in unusual cases, needs to be balanced".

- "In industry after industry, the central cause of the shift of American production and jobs to other countries is the difference in wage levels. Goods produced in low-wage nations undersell those produced in high-wage nations. That is the heart of the matter".

- "A drop in the dollar is not a way of curing our trade deficit without reducing our standard of living ... The reasonable objective of national policy has to be to correct the U.S. trade deficit in a way that does not reduce our wage level and our standard of living ... Thus, we need a new kind of trade policy that accepts the positive goal of assuring that the trade of the United States with other countries is in balance and is beneficial to the United States".

- "The major task ... would be to halt and in some cases reverse the increases in imports that have been causing the failures of U.S. firms and the loss of jobs in a number of industries ... The major tool would be quotas by type of good and by nation".

In short, the diagnosis is that unimpeded competition from low-wage countries, often exacerbated by aggressive industrial targeting,

---

3) It would be rather ironic, though, if the seeming ineffectiveness of exchange rate variations should in fact strengthen the protectionist case. For there is every indication that the recent increase in the number and coverage of quantitative import restrictions - by severing, or at least loosening, the link between exchange rates and import prices - is a major cause of the unusually weak response of trade flows to the fall of the dollar. On this point, see *Hooper/Mann* 1987.

has caused the loss of markets, high-wage jobs and external equilibrium in the United States. According to this argument, the time-honored *Ricardian* doctrine of comparative advantage and mutually beneficial trade has been proven wrong. The proposed solution is that trade policy take care of the trade problem.

In contrast to this view, the present paper argues that the massive global trade imbalances do not reflect any sudden breakdown of the world economy's basic allocation mechanisms, but rather the divergence of macroeconomic policies. In a world of highly integrated capital markets, the medium-term swings in trade balances and in the competitiveness of different countries' tradables industries are largely a consequence of shifting patterns of saving, investment and spending. Those who advocate trade policies to deal with these consequences succumb to a fallacy of composition by failing to see that what trade policy can achieve for any particular industry, it cannot attain for the economy as a whole. More specifically, *trade policy can control the volume of trade and it can control the composition of trade, but it cannot control the balance of trade.*

Section 2 of the paper develops a simple macroeconomic model for the medium-term determination of the trade balance, broadly outlining the logic behind the proposition advanced above. Section 3 addresses the role of trade policy in short-run macroeconomic management. Section 4 offers a summary of the paper and some conclusions.

2. International competitiveness and the balance of trade in the medium term

As pointed out above, the emergence of the huge U.S. trade deficit during the 1980s is the main source of the current protectionist mood in the United States. Although the deficit was initially seen as a consequence of the U.S. lead overcoming the worldwide 1982 recession, it has become clear by now that the imbalance has persisted well beyond the short run dissynchronization of business cycles across nations. Thus, an explanation must be found which looks beyond the short run. To make the point as effectively as possible, the following model depicts a two-country world, taking national income as predetermined along medium-term trends in both countries[4]. Equations (1) and (2) express the equilibrium conditions for the circular flow of income and expenditure at home and abroad, respectively, while equation (3) gives a simple representation of the international assets market equilibrium:

(1) $$S(r,G,t) - I(r) = CA(E,C,C^*,x)$$

(2) $$S^*(r^*,G^*,t^*) - I^*(r^*) = CA^*(E,C,C^*,x)$$

(3) $$r = r^* + \delta$$

The notation is as follows:

S	national saving
I	domestic investment
CA	current account
r	real interest rate
G	government spending
t	tax rate
E	real exchange rate
C	commercial policy variable
x	catch-all variable for 'other' proximate determinants of the current account (non-price competitiveness, productivity differentials, net foreign interest payments etc.)
δ	risk premium
*	asterisk denotes foreign variable

In both countries national saving is assumed to depend positively on the real interest rate and the tax rate, and negatively on government spending; investment is assumed to depend negatively on the real interest rate, and the *Marshall-Lerner* condition is assumed to hold. The assets market equation (3) allows for a risk premium causing deviations from strict real interest rate parity, but ignores the possibility of expected real exchange rate variations as implied, for example, by the intrinsic dynamics of the net foreign asset positions.

---

4) This should not be confused with a full-employment assumption. The point is merely that in the medium and long run, real income cannot be counted upon to play a major equilibrating role in the mutual adjustment of saving, investment and the current account. The model is discussed more fully in *Landmann* 1988.

Furthermore, the two income-expenditure equations are linked by the familiar condition that the two current account surpluses must add up to zero (if expressed in a common currency). As the equations make clear, this is tantamount to saying that the savings deficiency of one country must be financed by a savings surplus in the other.

Figure 2 visualizes the interaction of these equilibrium conditions. Upon substitution of equation (3) into the LHS of equation (2), the foreign savings surplus can be expressed as an increasing function of the domestic interest rate - the FSS schedule in the top panel of Figure 2. Likewise, the SGAP schedule depicts the excess of domestic investment over national saving in the home country as a decreasing function of the interest rate. In equilibrium, the interest rate has adjusted so as to bring these two flows into balance, thus determining the net lending (capital flow) between the two countries. In the bottom panel, the bilateral balance of the current account is related to the real exchange rate which serves as a measure of relative competitiveness (CAB schedule). The crucial point is the endogeneity of the exchange rate. Since the current account must equal the savings surplus, the latter being determined by spending patterns at home and abroad (as shown in the top panel), the exchange rate bears the burden of adjustment, bringing the current account into line with the net capital flow[5].

The model explains the medium-term effects of a shift in fiscal policy. Suppose we start at point A in both panels, with the home country current account slightly in surplus at the intersection of $SGAP_0$ and FSS. As the home country switches to a more expansionary fiscal policy, raising government expenditure and/or cutting taxes, the SGAP schedule moves to the right ($SGAP_1$). A new equilibrium is established in point B with higher interest rates worldwide and a net capital inflow to the home country. In order to accommodate the induced capital flow, the current account must move into deficit, with a real appreciation of the home currency serving as transmission belt (transition from A to B in the bottom panel).

---

[5]) Note that the logic of the model does not depend on the exchange rate regime under which the system is assumed to operate. The necessary adjustment of the real exchange rate may be thought to be brought about either by changes in relative price levels or by nominal exchange rate movements.

Figure 2: A Graphical Representation of the Medium-Term Two-Country Model

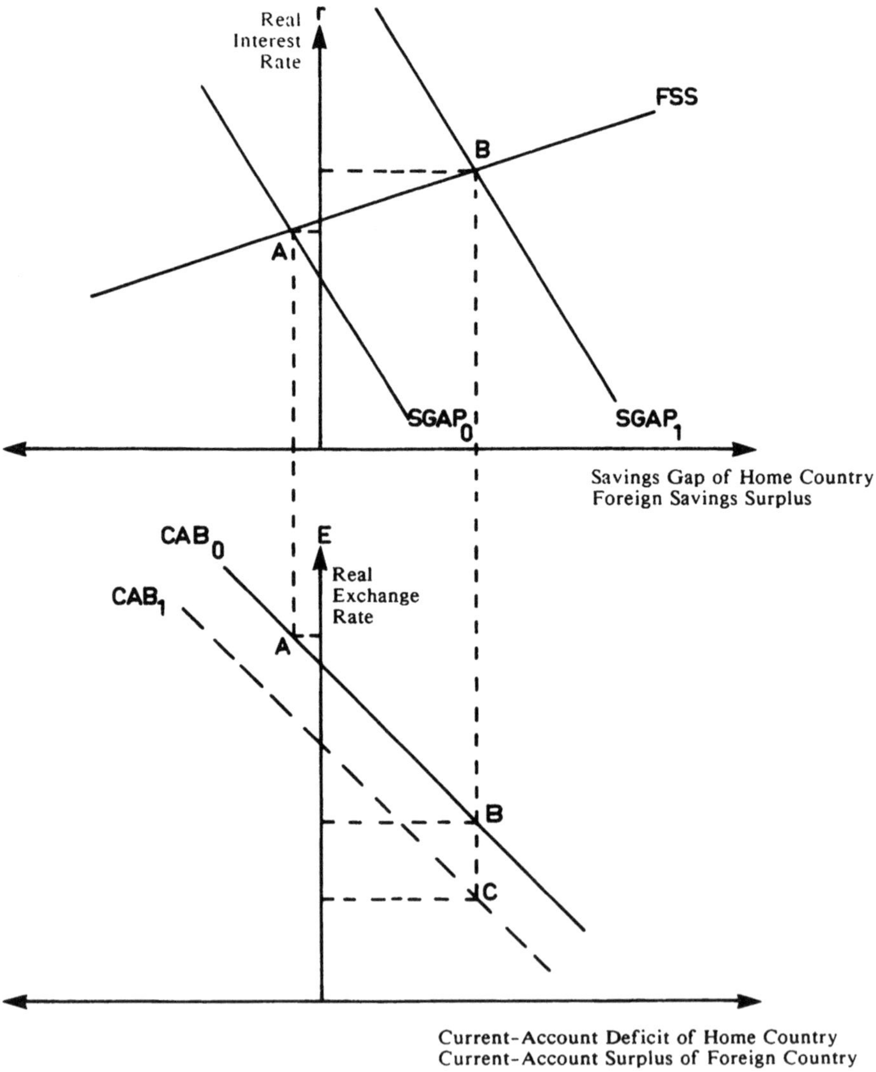

The story told by this model elucidates the role of the exchange rate in the process of fiscal crowding out. As the government and/or the taxpayers command a larger share of GNP, something has to give. To the extent that the interest rate rises, interest sensitive sectors such as housing will be hurt. The remaining excess demand is crowded out by real appreciation which squeezes resources out of the tradables sector. One should then not be surprised to hear manufacturing industries complain about foreign low-wage producers invading their markets, destroying well-paying jobs and eroding the home country's industrial base - because that is exactly what it means for them.

Can protection close the trade deficit and bring back those lost jobs? Obviously, the answer is no. Suppose the deficit country, finding itself in the undesirable position depicted by point B in both panels of Figure 2, decides to erect new trade barriers in order to stem the swelling flood of imports. There is no question that a higher level of net exports could now be achieved at any given real exchange rate, i. e. the CAB schedule in the bottom panel of Figure 2 shifts leftward (from CAB_0 to CAB_1). However, as long as saving and investment are not affected in at least one of the countries, the current-account deficit will not go away. Rather, the artificial boost to competitiveness will dissipate in further real appreciation, bringing the economy to point C in the bottom panel of Figure 2.

The logic behind this result is straightforward: as imports are curbed, the demand for foreign exchange falls, pushing the exchange rate down and thus exacerbating the plight of export-dependent industries and unprotected producers of import-substitutes. The tradables sector as a whole simply cannot attract additional resources unless they are released elsewhere in the economy. This analysis confirms one of the basic tenets of pure trade theory, known as *Lerner*'s symmetry theorem: A tariff on imports is equivalent to a tax on exports. Relative prices may be twisted in favor of any particular industry or even in favor of the import-competing sector as a whole, but that does not change the nature of the constant-sum game played by all tradables industries combined - "just as squeezing a balloon will redistribute but not reduce the total amount of air in the balloon" (*Lawrence/Litan* 1987, p. 296)[6].

---

6) There is ample empirical evidence of how protection in effect taxes exporters: for an instructive study, see *Clements/Sjaastad* 1984.

It should be noted, though, that there are a number of indirect channels by which commercial policy might affect the current account in the medium term. First of all, there is a rarely noticed *valuation effect*: This effect, which is not explicitly brought out by Figure 2, results from the condition that for the determination of the capital market equilibrium the domestic and foreign net supplies of savings must be expressed in the same currency units. Formally, the equilibrium condition represented in the top panel of Figure 2 is given by

$$(4) \qquad I - S = E \cdot (S^* - I^*)$$

if S^* and I^* are denominated in foreign currency units. As a consequence, the FSS schedule rotates anti-clockwise around its intercept as the imposition of import restrictions appreciates the home currency. This leads to a reduction of the existing imbalance[7].

A second channel worth mentioning is the possible existence of an *exchange rate effect on spending*. This effect played a major role in *Mundell*'s (1961) classic treatment of commercial policy under flexible exchange rates and it is again stressed today by *McKinnon* (1987) and others who dispute the efficacy of exchange rate changes as a cure for an external disequilibrium[8]. The theoretical foundation and empirical relevance of a terms-of-trade effect on spending has remained somewhat controversial to date. The classical *Laursen-Metzler* effect, in particular, hinges on a less than unit real income elasticity of aggregate spending and would thus appear to be of minor importance in the medium-term context that we consider in this section.

Thirdly, commercial policy might effect spending patterns by altering the *distribution of income*. As *Hufbauer* (1987, p. 344) observes:

> "A closed-market trade policy that avoids marginal cost pricing can powerfully protect business earnings. And such earnings are a mainspring of the Japanese *Keiretsu* system. If U.S. commercial policy could gain access for American goods to Japanese markets,

---

[7] Note, however, that the deficit increases if expressed in foreign currency units.

[8] The role of the exchange rate for aggregate investment demand is further discussed by Ryuhei *Okumura* in this volume.

that would not just enlarge U.S. exports. It would also shrink Japanese business savings".

This argument is fine as far as it goes. But it depends sensitively on the type of commercial policy pursued and on the type of labor market arrangements in force. There is little reason to presume that commercial policies actually implemented by the United States so far had much of an effect along these lines. While trade restraints certainly generated significant profits in protected industries, there is also much evidence that workers were able to appropriate a significant fraction of monopoly rents, especially in the steel and automobile industries (see *Crandall* 1987). On the other hand, these trade restraints hardly did much harm to foreign profits. In some instances of VERs, they may even have actively promoted oligopolistic coordination in heavily concentrated foreign export industries.

The most important and immediate link between commercial policy and national saving is established by the *revenue effect* of a tariff - or of a quota if it is auctioned off. As the government collects the revenue, it shrinks its budget deficit, thereby raising national saving. Of course, if that is the route by which the policy affects trade flows, the presumption is that a more broadly based tax increase would be vastly superior on welfare grounds. However, some U.S. economists such as *Branson* (1987), accepting that the optimal expenditure-reducing policy is not attainable politically, propose an across-the-board import surcharge as a second-best alternative, just for the sake of the revenue. Somehow paradoxically, this strategy looks all the more promising as the current persistence of the trade deficit seems to reflect a rather low price elasticity of imports, which is a favorable condition for raising revenue by means of a tariff. In contrast, the traditional partial equilibrium elasticities approach to the balance of trade would have suggested that a tariff is more successful in the face of highly elastic imports.

3. Short-run effects of commercial policy under flexible exchange rates

The logic of *Lerner*'s symmetry theorem which we have used above to explain the ineffectiveness of commercial policy in dealing with an external imbalance presupposes a fully employed economy. More accurately, it presupposes that a stimulus to aggregate demand does not draw additional resources into the production process. While this assumption is a reasonable starting point in a medium and long-term context, it may clearly be violated in the short run. In a *Keynes*ian underemployment situation, the expansion of import-competing sectors need not divert workers from export-dependent industries, but may rather draw upon the pool of the unemployed. Thus, commercial policy is able to produce an expansion of employment and an improvement of the external account at the same time. Because of this implication, the *Keynes*ian paradigm has often been accused of providing neomercantilism with an air of intellectual respectability. In fact, as is well known, *Keynes* himself favored protectionist policies to stimulate the British economy in 1930/31 - but only as a last resort, when his criticism of British exchange rate policy and his proposals for internationally coordinated demand expansion had failed to impress policymakers.

Under a fixed exchange rate, it can be unambiguously shown that a tariff or other forms of import restriction improve the balance of trade in a *Keynes*ian model. If the tariff revenue is redistributed in lump-sum form, output expands. If the revenue is retained, the output response depends on the price elasticity of imports. In contrast, *Mundell* (1961) has shown that under flexible exchange rates commercial policy leads to an appreciation strong enough to leave output and the balance of trade unaffected in the absence of a *Laursen-Metzler* effect. Thus *Lerner*'s symmetry theorem carries over to the *Keynes*ian short-run if the exchange rate is flexible. The logic of the argument is immediately evident from the structure of the standard *Mundell-Fleming* model:

$$Q = A(r,Q,G) + CA(E,Q,Q^*,C,C^*) \qquad \text{IS} \tag{5}$$

$$M = L(r,Q) \qquad \text{LM} \tag{6}$$

$$BOP = K(r-r^*) + CA(E,Q,Q^*,C,C^*) \qquad \text{BOP} \tag{7}$$

where Q is national income, A is absorption, M is money supply, BOP is balance of payments, and K is net capital inflow (other variables as above). In the case of a small open economy, foreign variables are exogenous. Exchange rate flexibility is defined by BOP

= 0. The commercial policy parameter C does not appear in the absorption function, which reflects *Mundell*'s assumption that there are no revenue effects. Upon substitution of equation (7) into equation (5), real output and the interest rate are readily seen to be determined independently of commercial policy. Thus, the impact of the latter on the current account must be fully offset by an exchange rate adjustment[9].

This ineffectiveness result was a major element in the intellectual case for flexible exchange rates towards the end of the Bretton Woods era. With the balance of payments automatically in equilibrium and the exchange rate swiftly neutralizing any protectionist moves, so the argument went, flexible exchange rates would eliminate politicians' bent for protection. Ironically, the flexible exchange rate system seems to have worked exactly in the opposite direction. As internationally exposed sectors experienced pronounced swings in their relative competitive position due to the cycles of currency depreciation and appreciation, the demand for protection increased[10].

Of course, exchange rate theory has evolved substantially in the more than 25 years since *Mundell* proved his ineffectiveness result. In particular, the asset market approach to exchange rate determination has gained general acceptance. As equation (7) above indicates, the *Mundell-Fleming* model represents a flexible exchange rate as proximately determined by the condition for a flow equilibrium on the foreign exchange market (CA = K). Thus, we might want to know whether *Mundell*'s result continues to hold once the exchange rate is depicted as determined by the conditions for an asset market equilibrium. As it turns out, this is not necessarily the case. Since the short-run asset market equilibrium is not directly affected by a shock to the current account, the exchange rate is not forced to adjust so far as to offset the shock completely, except in the limiting case of perfect asset substitutability.

A simple way to show this is to replace the balance-of-payments equation of the *Mundell-Fleming* model by the following

---

[9] If allowance is made for a *Laursen-Metzler* effect in the absorption function, the tariff-induced appreciation lowers aggregate demand, which in turn improves the current account. For a comprehensive discussion of commercial policy under fixed and flexible exchange rates, see *Tower* 1973.

[10] It should be noted, however, that *Dornbusch/Frankel* (1987) find little systematic evidence for a close link between exchange rate behavior and protection.

specification of a bonds market equilibrium:

$$(8) \qquad B = B(r, r^{*}, Q, W-M)$$

$$(9) \qquad W \equiv M + B + EF$$

where B is the stock of domestic bonds held by the public, F is the stock of foreign bonds held by the public, and W is total financial wealth. Equation (8) says that the demand for domestic bonds varies with domestic and foreign rates of return as well as with income and with non-monetary wealth. F is assumed positive, and in order to facilitate the comparison with the *Mundell-Fleming* framework, expectations are assumed static. The wealth constraint (9) makes a separate equilibrium conditon for foreign bonds redundant, but imposes some adding-up constraints on the partial derivatives of the demand functions for money and domestic bonds:

$$(10) \qquad B_r > - L_r > 0; \quad L_Q > - B_Q > 0 \qquad 0 < B_W < 1$$

We are now in a position to solve for the exchange rate effect of commercial policy. In the *Mundell-Fleming* case - equations (5) - (7)-, we get

$$(11) \qquad \left.\frac{dE}{dC}\right|_{MF} = - \frac{CA_C}{CA_E} < 0,$$

(Mundell-Fleming)

which implies an exchange rate adjustment strong enough to leave the current account unchanged.

Using the portfolio balance specification (5) - (6) and (8) - (9), in contrast, we get

$$(12) \qquad \left.\frac{dE}{dC}\right|_{PB} = - \frac{CA_C}{CA_E + \dfrac{FB_W\{A_r L_Q + L_r(1 - A_Q - CA_Q)\}}{L_r B_Q - B_r L_Q}}$$

(Portfolio Balance specification)

Taking account of the adding-up constraints (10), it is immediately evident that the portfolio balance specification predicts an appreciation in response to a protectionist policy as well, but that this appreciation is smaller than in the *Mundell-Fleming* case. Thus the current account improves and output expands. Only in the limiting case of perfect asset substitutability ($B_r \rightarrow \infty$) is the appreciation large enough to offset the impact of commercial policy on the current account. In this special case, (12) obviously coincides with (11).

A major insight of the asset market approach to exchange rate determination concerns the role of expectations, which we have so far neglected by assuming static expectations. We will not be surprised, then, to find that the effect of commercial policy sensitively depends on how it affects expectations. The simplest way to demonstrate this point is to consider the consequences of a tariff within the standard rational-expectations overshooting model as developed by *Dornbusch* (1976)[11]. Writing the model in log-linear form, with lower case variables denoting logs except in the case of interest rates, we have

(13) $q = \alpha_0 e^r - \alpha_1 r + \alpha_2 c$ output determination

(14) $m - p = \beta_0 q - \beta_1 (r + \dot{p})$ money market equilibrium

(15) $r = r^* + \dot{e}^r$ perfect capital mobility

(16) $\dot{p} = \pi (q - \bar{q})$ price level inertia

The notation is as usual. In addition to the variables already introduced above, we have the (logs of the) real exchange rate e^r, the price level p and the long-run equilibrium (natural) output q. Dots denote time derivatives. Since we continue to focus on the pure substitution effect of commercial policy, disregarding revenue or income effects, α_2 is unambiguously positive. The long-run effects of commercial policy are easily derived by setting

$\dot{e}^r = \dot{p} = 0$:

(17) $$\frac{de^r}{dc} = - \frac{\alpha_2}{\alpha_0} \quad \text{and} \quad \frac{dq}{dc} = 0,$$

---

[11] This approach is also taken by *Dornbusch* (1987), who chooses to emphasize different issues, however.

which confirms our conclusion in section 2 that commercial policy measures are fully absorbed by real exchange rate adjustments, thus leaving output, employment and the current account unchanged.

The short-run dynamics of the model are illustrated in Figure 3, with the $e^r = 0$ and $p = 0$ loci and the saddle-path SP derived in the standard way. The effect of commercial policy can be represented by a vertical displacement of the model's long-run equilibrium position (e.g. from A to B) because the equilibrium price level only depends on the money supply, the foreign interest rate and natural output, which remain all unchanged. Analyzing the short-run impact of the policy, we find that the economy moves to its new long-run equilibrium at once if the change is unanticipated and permanent. Starting from point A, the real exchange rate must immediately jump onto the saddle-path SP, and since the equilibrium price level remains unchanged, the point first reached on the saddle-path coincides with the new long-run equilibrium[12]. Thus, the result derived above within the *Mundell-Fleming* model is upheld in the perfect-capital-mobility rational expectations framework. It critically depends on the permanent character of the policy change and the implied revision of exchange rate expectations. If agents are not confident that the policy change is permanent or for other reasons fail to revise their long-run exchange rate expectations by the full amount given in (17), the short-run response of the exchange rate falls short of fully neutralizing the change in commercial policy. In this case policymakers are able to achieve the hoped for effects on output and the current account, at least in the short run.

As a further result, therefore, we find that commercial policies have a better chance of delivering the desired macroeconomic results if they are explicitly announced as temporary emergency measures. The dynamic response of the system to temporary import restrictions is indicated in the upper panel of Figure 3 by the sequence A → C → D → A[13]. It is assumed that AB would represent the equilibrium exchange rate adjustment if the policy change were believed to be permanent. This cannot be the response of the exchange rate in the

---

[12] It should be noted that this analysis ignores the lag in the response of the current account to a change in the exchange rate (J-Curve).

[13] Analytically, a temporary policy change can be treated as a permanent policy change, augmented by an anticipated future policy change in reverse direction. The analysis of anticipated shocks in a *Dornbusch*-type exchange rate model was pioneered by *Wilson* (1979).

Figure 3: The Effects of Permanent and Temporary Import Restrictions under Rational Expectations

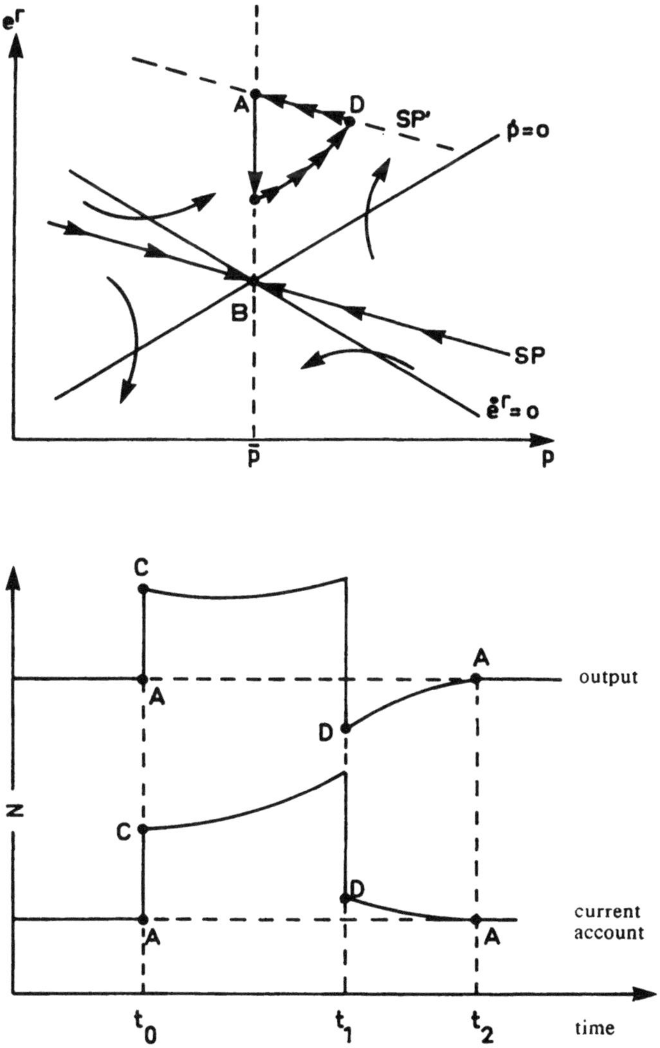

Top panel: The dynamics of the real exchange rate and the price level in the cases of permanent protection (A →B) and temporary protection (A→C →D →A).

Bottom panel: The dynamic adjustment of real output and the current account in the case of temporary protection (capital letters indicate identical situations in both panels).

event of a temporary policy change because it would require the exchange rate to jump back to A once the trade restrictions are lifted again, thus opening up an opportunity for large anticipated speculative profits. In fact, these profits are arbitraged away on the foreign exchange market. The resulting short-run arbitrage equilibrium is given by point C where the system is temporarily placed on an explosive time path. Point D is reached just when the temporary policy change is reversed. The equilibrium position is now given by point A again, and the system moves toward that equilibrium along the unique convergent saddle-path SP'.

The implications of this dynamic adjustment pattern for the level of economic activity and the current account are outlined in a stylized way in the bottom panel of Figure 3. At time t_0, the protectionist policy is introduced. Because of its temporary character, the response of the real exchange rate is limited (to AC in the top panel) so as to allow the current account and real output to improve (by AC in the bottom panel). Until time t_1, when the policy is reversed, the current account continues to improve because the real exchange rate is depreciating and the real interest rate is rising (which curbs domestic demand and thus contributes to current-account improvement)[14]. When the protection is taken away at time t_1, real output and the current account fall sharply. Notably, they fall by more than they increased at time t_0 because this time the policy change was anticipated and, therefore, is not accompanied by a cushioning jump in the real exchange rate. The economy now finds itself in a recession from which it gradually recovers as the price level and the real interest rate fall while the real exchange rate and real output rise to reach their initial equilibrium values at time t_2 (point A in both panels)[15].

It cannot be overemphasized that our model provides but a stylized account of the dynamics. In particular, the uncertainty that inevitably will surround the duration of any protectionist policy and the lags associated with the policy itself as well as with the induced exchange rate movements are likely to 'round off' the sharp corners in the time

14) The real depreciation can be directly inferred from the top panel, the rise of the real interest rate indirectly by noting that the path from C to D leads away from the $\dot{e}^r = 0$ locus. The latter can be interpreted as an iso-real-interest-rate locus as long as the foreign interest rate is given (cf. Equation (15) above).

15) Whether or not the current account falls below its initial level at time t_1 is uncertain. Figure 3 assumes it does not.

path of the current account and real output. The main point is that expectational effects of the kind described above are a major factor affecting the short-run macroeconomic effects of protectionist policies under flexible exchange rates. Of course, such expectational effects can show up in various and sometimes perhaps surprising ways. For example, protectionist measures are rarely introduced suddenly and entirely unexpectedly, but are more often preceded by a lengthy political decision-making process. Asset markets are then likely to respond before the policy actually takes effect.

Things are further complicated if the threat of protection generates major repercussions on other branches of policy-making, at home or abroad. This type of indirect causation has been nicely illustrated by the distinct announcement effects recorded on foreign exchange markets whenever the U.S. Congress made an important step towards some protectionist legislation in recent years. Regularly, the U.S. dollar dropped significantly against major foreign currencies. This may seem to stand in puzzling contrast to the above analysis which indicated that protection should lead to an appreciation of the home currency. There are two explanations: Either the markets anticipated major income effects of the proposed legislation, in which case it is conceivable that the equilibrium value of the dollar would have had to fall. However, considering the nature of the legislation under discussion - mostly non-auctioned import quotas -, this explanation lacks plausibility. More likely, financial markets were aware that monetary policymakers at home and abroad as well as the executive branch of government had a keen interest in avoiding any protectionist escalation and would, therefore, be quick to put more pressure on the dollar in order to placate and weaken the forces lobbying for protection. The mere expectation of such a policy response was enough to push the dollar down.

4. Summary and conclusions

In the past fifteen years we have witnessed a significant slowdown, if not reversal of the momentum of trade liberalization that had marked the 1950s and 1960s. While the deterioration of the macroeconomic environment is in all likelihood a major cause of this development, most of the new protectionism was motivated by industrial policy concerns rather than macroeconomically. This began to change in the 1980s when the U.S. balance of trade moved into deficit on an unprecedented scale. As the American manufacturing sector was hard hit by the sky-high dollar and by the LDC debt crisis, strong pressure built up to solve the problem by 'stemming the flood of imports'.

The main message of the present paper is contained in section 2: The global trade imbalances and currency misalignments of the 1980s were not caused by any sudden malfunctioning of the international trading system, which would require some sort of 'trade management', but rather by a divergence of macroeconomic policies in the United States and in the rest of the OECD area. To cure the resulting disequilibria, a reversal of these macroeconomic developments is required. Protectionist policies are inherently unable to solve the problem. They achieve little else than a redistribution of the hardship among industries.

Is it conceivable that the ardent advocates of protection fail to grasp this simple and basic lesson of economics? At times, one might suspect it is. But, of course, on a more fundamental level we have to take into account the political economy of protectionism. Even though commercial policies may fail to achieve anything macroeconomically, they have powerful effects on individual industries. And this is where the pressure comes from. The highly concentrated, extremely visible and well organized interests suffering from foreign competition by far outweigh the diffuse, invisible and poorly organized interests suffering from protection. And even if a pressure group is fully aware that its problems stem from misguided macroeconomic policies rather than from 'unfair' foreign competition, its cost-benefit analysis is likely to indicate that the expected payoff to lobbying for protection is much higher and much more certain than the payoff to lobbying for sound fiscal policies.

What, after all this, remains of the macroeconomic case for protection? There are three arguments to be considered. First, one might argue that protectionist policies improve the short-run trade-off between internal and external equilibrium. We have seen in section 3 that this argument cannot easily be dismissed under flexible exchange rates in the way *Mundell*'s original analysis had suggested. If assets denominated in different currencies are less than perfect substitutes or if trade barriers are not thought to remain in place permanently, the exchange rate does not immediately appreciate enough to offset the entire impact of commercial policy on the current account and on real output. However, one should bear in mind that any current-account improvement brough about by means of protection cannot last, failing a correction of the underlying savings deficit. Quite to the contrary, if the artificial and temporary boost to the tradables sector delays action to tackle the real cause of the problem, it is outright counter-productive.

A second line of argument suggests that import restrictions are the only politically feasible way for the government to raise the revenue required to reduce its budget deficit. The much more serious distortions that result from raising a given revenue from the narrow base of foreign trade rather than from a broader income or spending base would then have to be regarded as the premium the political system puts on choosing the way of minimum resistance. Of course, the successive lowering of tariffs and the concomitant spread of non-tariff-barriers have taken out most of the fascination that protectionism once had for finance ministers. Most quotas are still not auctioned off, after all. Some economists tend to argue, therefore, that existing quotas at least should be auctioned if they cannot be avoided. But in fact it is hard to see why our profession should teach politicians how to make unsound policies even more attractive politically than they already are, instead of pointing out the irrationality and the misconceptions involved.

The third argument starts from the recognition that an external disequilibrium will not go away unless domestic spending is reduced, but that an expenditure switching mechanism is required nevertheless. As we have seen in section 2, this expenditure switching is ordinarily ensured by adjustments in the real exchange rate. The correction of an external deficit thus requires a real depreciation. This depreciation, and the real income loss that goes with it, could be avoided if appropriate commercial policies were adopted instead[16]. While a tariff does not contribute to the improvement of the trade balance in the long run (unless the revenue is retained by the government), it can save the income that would otherwise be transferred abroad by the terms-of-trade loss. Of course, this is basically the optimum tariff argument, long known to trade theorists, and it has gained importance in the current debate over US trade policy as consumers increasingly feel the pinch of a lower dollar (again, see *Culbertson* 1987).

---

16) In terms of Figure 2, the exchange rate change which takes place along the CAB schedule as the savings-investment balance is adjusted, could be avoided if commercial policy shifts the CAB schedule accordingly.

Perhaps, this optimum tariff argument shows most clearly what is wrong with the protectionist argument. The manipulation of the terms of trade for the sake of real income gains is an international conflict strategy par excellence. As such, it invites retaliation and is thus unlikely to be optimal in any meaningful sense once all repercussions are taken into account. There is much talk of international policy coordination nowadays. Nobody knows exactly what this is supposed to mean in practice. But if it is to mean anything, it certainly requires that countries refrain from conflict strategies such as protection.

References

Branson, W., Comment on Macroeconomics and Protection, in R. *Stern* (ed.), U.S.Trade Policies in a Changing Economy, MIT Press 1987, pp. 131-36

Clements, K./*Sjaastad*, L., How Protection Taxes Exporters, Thames Essay No. 39, Trade Policy Research Centre, London 1984

Crandall, R., The Effects of the U.S. Trade Protection for Autos and Steel, Brookings Papers on Economic Activity, 1, 1987, pp. 271-288

Culbertson, J., Toward a Realistic Trade Policy, Economic Impact, 4, 1987, pp. 51-57

Dornbusch, R., Expectations and Exchange Rate Dynamics, Journal of Political Economy, 84, 1976, pp. 1161-76

Dornbusch, R., External Balance Correction: Depreciation or Protection?, Brookings Papers on Economic Activity, 1, 1987, pp. 249-270

Dornbusch, R./*Frankel*, J., Macroeconomics and Protection, in R. *Stern* (ed.), U.S. Trade Policies in a Changing Economy, MIT Press 1987

Hooper, P./*Mann*, C., The U.S. External Deficit: Its Causes and Persistence, International Finance Discussion Paper No. 316, Board of Governors of the Federal Reserve System, Washington, November 1987

Hufbauer, G., Comment, Brookings Papers on Economic Activity, 1, 1987, pp. 337-45

Krueger, A., Prospects for Liberalizing the International Trading System, in: S. *Borner* (ed.), International Finance and Trade in a Polycentric World, IEA conference volume, London 1988

Landmann, O., Current Issues in the International Macroeconomic Policy Debate, in: S. *Borner* (ed.), International Finance and Trade in a Polycentric World, IEA conference volume, London 1988

Lawrence, R./*Litan*, R., The Protectionist Prescription: Errors in Diagnosis and Cure, Brookings Papers on Economic Activity, 1, 1987, pp. 289-310

McKinnon, R., Currency Protection: Parity Lost, The Wall Street Journal, February 3, 1987

Mundell, R., Flexible Exchange Rates and Employment Policy, Canadian Journal of Economics and Political Science, 27, 1961, pp. 509-17

Tower, E., Commercial Policy under Fixed and Flexible Exchange Rates, Quarterly Journal of Economics, 87, 1973, pp. 436-54

Wilson, Ch., Anticipated Shocks and Exchange Rate Dynamics, Journal of Political Economy, 87, 1979, pp. 639-47

The Industrial Policy of Japan

Takashi Matsugi

1. Introduction

In the history of Japanese economic development since the Meiji Restoration, industrial policy played a key role. In a sense it can be said that the main objective was how to increase exports in order to procure foreign currencies and to import capital goods for industrialization. In a rough survey, the items to be exported were agricultural products in the last decades of the nineteenth century, manufactures of light industry in the first half of this century and those of heavy industry in the past thirty years.

Industrial policy is understood in the broad sense as policies in general concerning industries, but in the narrower sense it is defined as a set of policies concerning manufacturing which have anything to do with resource allocation and affect industrial organization[1]. In Japan, it is commonly agreed that the Ministry of International Trade and Industry (MITI) is responsible for it. Concrete examples are construction of infrastructures such as industrial sites, roads, harbors, water supply, electric power supply and so on.

In the following sections, topics selected are industrial policies in the time of rapid economic growth, the recent policy stance of MITI, the import promotion of foreign manufactured goods, and the agricultural policy for the adjustment to import liberalization.

2. A brief survey of Japanese industrial policy in 1960-1980

Japanese industrial policy today is faced with problems which have resulted from huge trade surpluses accumulated in recent years. More

---

[1] Cf. *Komiya* (ed.) 1984, pp. 3-6.

concretely they focus on how to solve conflicts with trade partners and how to adjust to the high appreciation of the yen. There are many arguments about solutions of which the basic one is recognized as the restructuring of Japanese industries with a view to improve the Japanese trade balance[2].

After World War II, the Japanese economy for a long time suffered from trade deficits as the ceiling of economic growth. In order to raise this ceiling, it was necessary to strengthen the competitiveness of Japanese industries in the world market and to increase exports from Japan. It was then pursued both at the micro and at the macro level to achieve strong competitiveness. The economic causation was followed in the line of technological progress, investment in plant and equipment, higher labor productivity and strong competitiveness.

2.1. Active investments in plant and equipment in the time of rapid economic growth

The economic policy of the 1960s, known as the "Income Doubling Plan", aimed to encourage the development of such key industries as iron and steel, electric machinery and automobiles and to realize the economic growth led by active investments in plant and equipment in these industries. The high income elasticity of comodities was taken into consideration as investment criterion at that time. These investments introduced new technologies in plants, reduced production costs and improved the quality of products to the extent that Japanese exports started to increase through enhanced competitiveness. The Japanese economy at that time was characterized by excess supply of labor and excess demand for capital. Monetary policy then supported bankers to give credits to industries to meet their financial requirements, but the state of excess loans lasted long. It was significantly estimated in empirical studies of the investment function that private investments were elastic to the rate of interest.

These investments raised labor productivity and increased personal income, so that private consumption correspondingly contributed to economic growth. Technologies introduced at that time were mostly imported from abroad. Therefore Japan was dependent on foreign countries in procurement not only of natural resources but also of advanced technologies.

---

[2] A typical example is the *Maekawa* Report.

2.2. Pollution as a price for economic growth

Production capacity of Japan was raised and the standard of living was improved through active investments in the time of rapid economic growth. However, not much attention was paid to the quality of environment; and industrial wastes tended to aggravate environmental conditions, threatening the security of human life. The price for economic growth had to be paid in terms of increasing damage to the environment and diseases caused by pollution.

In order to tackle pollution problems, the Basic Anti-Pollution Law was enacted in 1967 and the principle of polluter responsibility became effective. Accordingly, investment for waste disposal was increased. This kind of investment did not raise production capacity, but merely raised the capital-output ratio to some degree. Technologies to control automobile exhaust have been developed since then. One should note that regulations on air pollution are prevailing in the United States and Europe, for public concern about global threats to environment, such as acid rain, is mounting. The anti-pollution technology developed in the past would help Japanese automakers deal with regulations on exhaust emission in the US and in the EC car market.

2.3. Energy saving efforts after the oil shock in 1973

The oil shock in 1973 inevitably caused industries to adjust to the unprecedented rise in energy prices. Efforts made in research and development for energy saving technologies gradually bore fruit and resulted in the reduction not only of unit energy input but also of total energy consumption. MITI supported "The Sunshine Plan" and "The Moonlight Plan" and promoted research to discover oil substitutes and to invent energy saving devices.

In the second half of the 1970s, developments became remarkable in the field of high technology such as in the areas of microelectronics and office automation. These new technologies brought about great changes in industrial production. The development of computers and new materials made products lighter, thinner, shorter and smaller. Robotics were first introduced by small and medium size firms which had difficulty in hiring a sufficient number of skilled workers. Today, it is not rare to see fully automated plants in operation.

The computer industry in Japan started to develop later than in the United States. In the earlier stage of development, it was under government protection as an infant industry. This protective policy was adopted as a counterbalancing power against the monopolistic position of IBM. Through the development of high technology, Japanese industries increasingly became internationally competitive, but increasing exports raised new problems such as trade conflicts.

It is a necessity for Japan to promote technological progress, because Japan as a country poor in natural resources has to depend on imports of primary products for which it must always consider what to export. In this sense, technological development is a strategic policy for Japan to survive in competition with both developed and developing countries. It goes without saying that private sectors primarily are responsible for research and development and that government should take appropriate policy measures where the market mechanism does not work effectively.

3. The recent policy stance of MITI[3]

Since the "*Maekawa* Report" was published, the Japanese economy has been going through a structural adjustment process, aiming to recover the balance of payments. The rectification of the external imbalance is the greatest concern of MITI, and another target, such as the improvement of the quality of life, seems to be secondary for the time being, so that it deserves only brief mention. MITI is expecting an "improvement", i.e. a reduction in the trade surplus of Japan, within five years. The reasons, why it would take so long to achieve an equilibrium in the balance of payments, are twofold according to the explanations made by MITI. They are the J-curve effect on the one hand and the substantial decrease of oil-prices on the other.

In place of decreasing exports, domestic demand should be activated and contribute to economic growth. Housing loans were made more easily available, both by means of an upper limit of credits and a monetary policy which lowered interests rates. As a result, investments in housing construction were stimulated very

---

[3] This section is based on the summary paper written by Mr. Ulrich *Schmid* as to the interview with the MITI on March 22, 1988.

much in 1987 and 1988. At the same time, excess liquidity due to the trade surplus brought a boom in the stock market and gave rise to speculations in the real estate market. The correspondingly increased capital gains realized in the two markets positively affected propensity to consume and played the same role as foreign demand had done in preceding years.

One should note that the lower interest rate affected domestic demand in such an indirect way that it raised the value of land. The consequence was that companies which possessed land as real estate were estimated higher in value and, as a result, their shares were priced higher in the stock market. This in turn increased the creditworthiness of companies and enabled them to take up credits for the purpose of investment.

MITI is not always pleased to hear that the industrial policy of Japan is comparatively succcessful and that the so-called "Japan Incorporated" is not a myth. It denies the reality of "Japan Incorporated" and emphasizes the ability of private enterprises to adjust to any changing circumstances. But it is not a mere exaggeration that one of the reasons for the recent increase in domestic demand has been the confidence on the part of the business sector in the economic policy of the government.

Japanese managers have gained some self-confidence in coping with the highly appreciated yen in the course of about two years since the fall of 1985. The first target for rationalization was set at the exchange rate of 170 yen against the dollar; but today, the target is set at around 140 yen in most cases and some ambitious managers are thinking of an exchange rate a bit lower than 140 yen. Companies have been reacting by means of buying cheaper half-manufactured goods from abroad and by investing more in foreign subsidiaries. It was no longer so important just to cut costs in their own production. The overseas production ratio of Japanese companies was about 4 % in 1987, being very low when compared with 20 %, for instance, in the case of West Germany. It can be said that there would still be a great deal of potential for further foreign direct investments in the future. Commodity imports in general were increasing substantially, as was pointed out by MITI. But the United States raised the question whether export prices of Japan rose as much as expected, by indicating the statistical evidence that they did not go up in dollar terms. As is shown in Figure 1, the export price index rose from 100.5 at the end of 1985 to 134.7 at the end of 1987, while the inter-

Figure 1: Trends in Japanese Exports

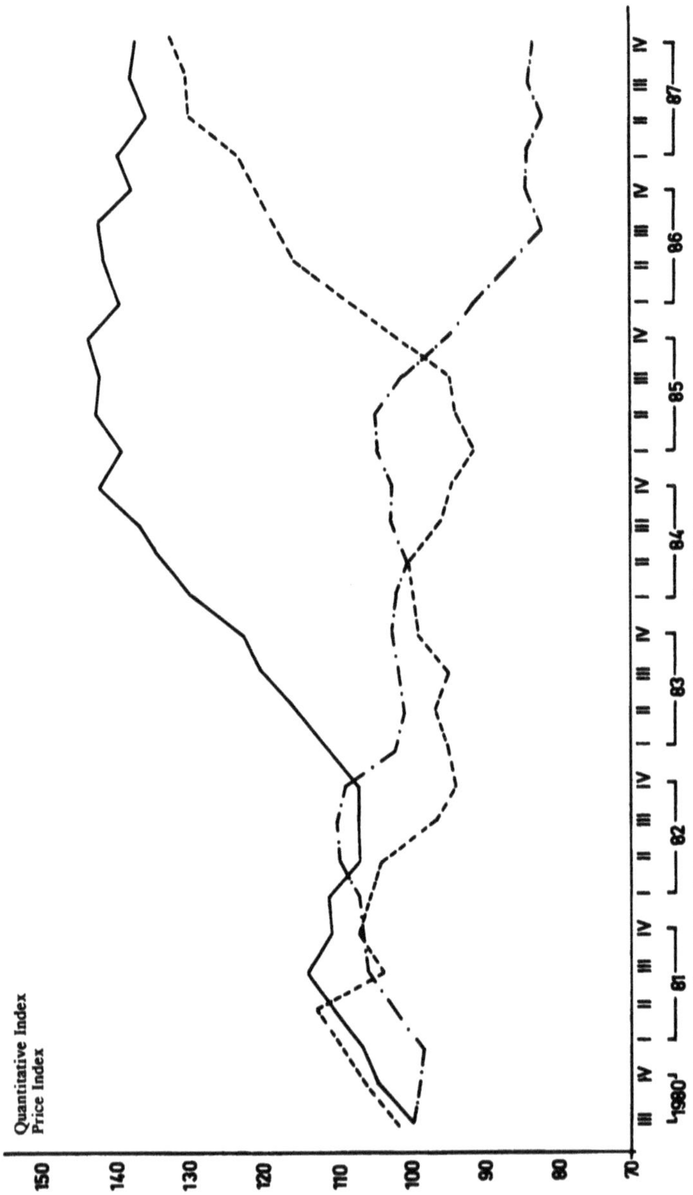

——— Export Quantitative Index 1980 = 100 seasonnally adjusted

– – – – Export Price Index (dollar term) 1980 = 100 actual

—·—·— Export Price Index (yen term) 1980 = 100 actual

Source : MOF, Foreign Trade Statistics

bank rates of the yen against the US dollar changed from 202.75 in December 1985 to 128.25 in December 1987. MITI insisted that the Japanese statistics were reliable and that attention should be paid to the following facts: (1) Imported raw materials became greatly cheaper in yen term, (2) Japanese manufacturers tried to keep their export prices as low as possible through cost reduction in spite of the yen appreciation. For example, after the dumping issues by the EC Commission against Japanese exporters of typewriters, they made attempts to reduce costs of production and supply their products almost at the same price (in European currencies) as before. This was meant to satisfy the European customers who would be willing to buy their products, if the price would remain as reasonable as before in relation to quality. (See also Figure 2 as for the import price index.)

4. Import promotion and related problems[4]

4.1. Changing roles of trade in Japanese economic development

In the early stage of the economic development, demands for imports such as machines, industrial intermediate products and weapons were very large. These goods were needed in order to start industrialization and to arrange military power. Foreign currencies necessary for these imports were limited in amount, so that export had to be promoted on the one hand, and imports of luxurious consumption goods were regulated on the other hand. Main exports at that time were tea, silk and its products, and mineral products.

Japan was not rich in natural resources, so the next strategy for economic development was to import cotton, iron ores and crude oil, to produce cotton textiles, steel products and chemicals, and to export some of them. Modern technologies needed for the development of these industries were also imported from developed countries. Several textile and steel plants were established and began operation as state owned enterprises.

Since more than half of the production capacities in basic industries were destroyed during World War II, the industrial policy

[4] This section is based on the presentation made by Mr. Kunio *Yagi*, Director of the Manufactured Imports Promotion Organization (MIPRO), in the symposium on "Protectionism or Liberalism?" held in Nagoya on March 26, 1988.

Figure 2: Trends in Japanese Imports

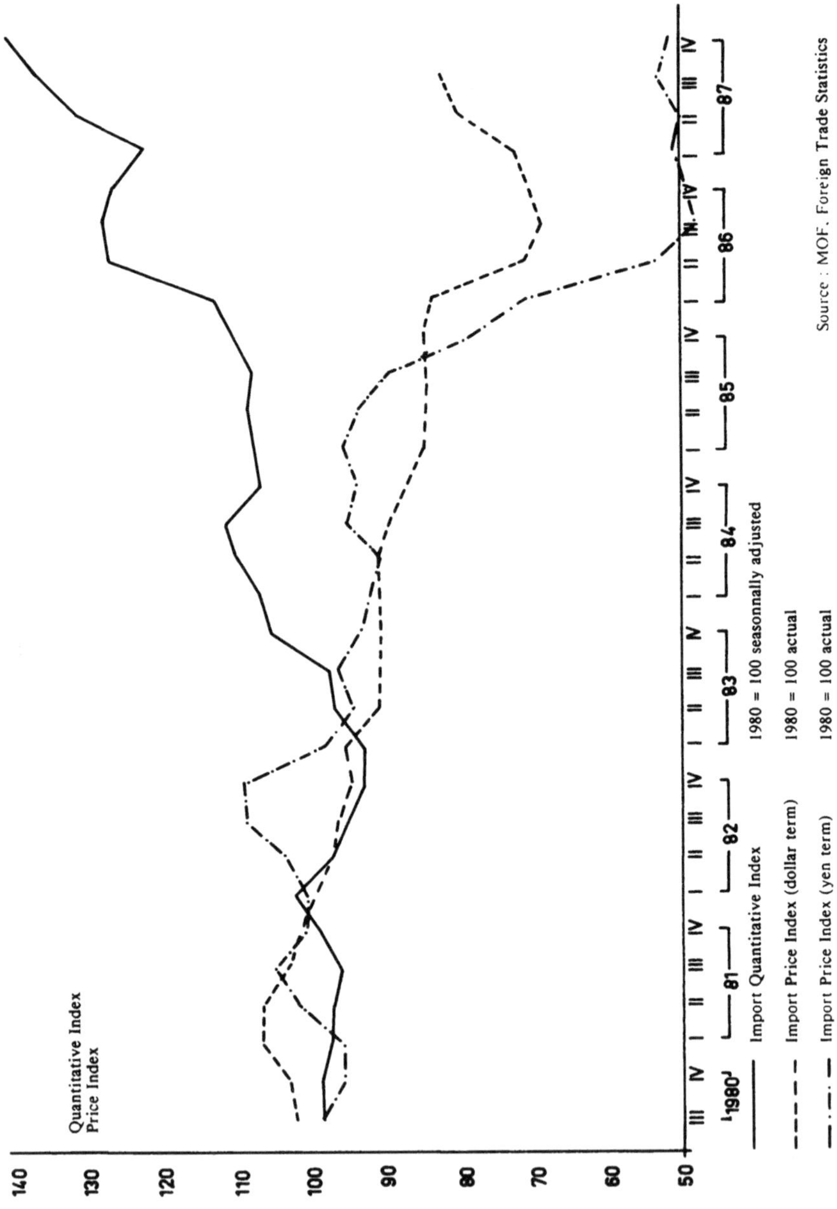

with the target "to export for import" was adopted once again as in the Meiji time, because imports of basic industrial products were urgently needed for the economic restoration in the postwar period. Policy menus were multiple and included the following goals: (1) the vertical international division of labor, namely to produce all goods in Japan except inevitable imports such as raw materials and manufacturing machines, (2) the principle of one-set production inside the country for import substitution, and (3) the promotion of exports of manufactured products to obtain foreign currency. Corresponding to these policies, investments were made in improvement of harbors, construction of industrial sites at the seashore, development of overseas resources, and encouragement of import substitution by introducing technologies from abroad. Furthermore, the action of "Buy Japanese" was spread under the slogan "I prefer the Japanese brand, because it is good", and imports of luxurious consumption goods were regarded as unnecessary and regulated by applying quotas and high tariffs.

These efforts in the 1960s were about to bear fruit and the trade balance was changing from deficit to surplus at the beginning of the 1970s, when the first oil shock upset the Japanese economy. Then, the rationalization policy was chosen and the development of production technologies, which saved energy and reduced costs, was promoted. In the following years, domestic demands were suppressed and financial reconstruction was aimed at, so that an export drive was necessary to cope with the depression. A favorable condition was provided from abroad at that time, because the US economy was in boom and there was the policy for a strong dollar. Japanese exporters, of whom automobile and electric appliance makers were typical examples for strong competitiveness, made the most of this chance. The time of "export for import" passed and the time of "growth based on export" followed. As a consequence, shares of exporting industries were one third to one half of the rate of economic growth, one half of investments in plant and equipment and one half of increases in industrial production. Only 10 % of large companies shared 90 % of Japanese exports.

In the meantime, the trade surplus amounted to US$ 44.3 billion in 1984, US$ 56.0 billion in 1985 and then even to US$ 92.8 billion in 1986 and US$ 96.5 billion in 1987. The stage of "import for export" was suddenly over and Japan was obliged to promise to the world "to rectify the disequilibrium in the balance of payments by increasing imports" or "to attain the balanced growth of the world economy by increasing manufactured goods imports from abroad". Corresponding policy measures were taken, such as the opening of the Japanese market in several steps and carrying out a comprehensive economic policy. The campaign for import promotion was also started under the slogan "International cooperation through import promotion".

During this time, exports of Asian NIEs were increasing, the yen was highly appreciated after the Plaza agreement in the fall of 1985, the US dollar continued to lose its value and Japan's imports of manufactured goods from abroad increased considerably. In spite of these facts, however, policy efforts did not bring about a sufficient reduction in the trade surplus, nor in capital outflows.

The price mechanism working through the strong yen and the weak dollar forced Japanese industries "to co-exist with other countries by increasing imports" and "to make profits by utilizing cheaper imports". At the same time, consumers were keen to benefit from declining import prices which should have been reflected in consumer prices and became more conscious about the internationally high relative price level in Japan.

4.2. The changing paradigm of trade

The tendency for imports of manufactures to increase and to gain in shares in production and distribution made the vertical international division of labor rather meaningless. Industrial statistics should reflect the changing structure of commodity flows by sector and by item, because shares of imported raw materials and parts, as well as of imported finished goods, will be rising.

There is a tendency for Japanese firms to become multinational and increasingly localize their production abroad. This makes it necessary to rearrange industrial statistics in order to understand adequately what is happening in the world economy. Examples are: increasing reimports of overseas products, enlargement of trilateral trade, growing importance of service trade, rising labor mobility. All in all, the Japanese economy is going to be borderless.

Considerations were taken to promote regional development by investing in local infrastructure. Harbors and related facilities were improved by investing tens of trillions of yen, so that imports of raw materials became possible for local use. These enabled imports of raw materials to amount to 6 trillion tons, of which 0.6 trillion tons were exported with value added. The rest was partly consumed and partly accumulated as waste which aggravated environmental problems.

As for the import of manufactures, concentrations were observed in certain regions where access to large markets was easy or airports were available. Improvements of local airports are regarded necessary, but only few investments have been made for that purpose. In addition, customs offices and inspection spots are not enough to import sufficient amounts of overseas manufactures for local use. It is reported that the transportation cost between Europe and Tokyo or Osaka is larger than that from there to local cities by domestic transport facilities.

5. Agricultural policy up to the year 2000[5]

5.1. Review of agricultural policy up to 1980

Agricultural policy in general aims at solving current agricultural problems at each stage. It may be successful in solving a problem in the short run, but after the solution, the next problem will appear which might not always be compatible with the successful result in the former stage. In the decade after World War II, Japan suffered much from food shortage and the most urgent policy was to increase food production. This policy was successful in the sense that the self-sufficiency ratio of rice was maintained to be nearly 100 %. In the same period, rice consumption tended to decrease gradually and rice surplus was foreseen to appear in coming years. Another good result was attained in nutrition intakes[6]. The per capita daily calorie intake of the Japanese increased continuously from 2,290 kcal in 1960 to the record-high level of 2,522 kcal in 1973. Since then, the figure decreased a little and has remained at the level of about 2,500 kcal until today. As for the PFC (protein, fats and carbohydrate) ratios of the Japanese people, they were P 12 %, F 12 % and C 76 % in 1960, while they changed to P 13 %, F 25 % and C 62 % in 1979. This change was realized, however, by importing feed grains and raising livestock and poultry so that the average self-sufficiency ratio for grains declined to 33 % in 1979 (69 % for food grains and only 2 % for feed grains).

---

[5] This section is based on the presentation made by Mr. Tetsuro *Yakushiji*, Vice-Director of Planning Division, International Affairs Department of the Ministry of Agriculture, Forestry and Fisheries, in the symposium mentioned above.

[6] See *Konosu* 1982, p. 12.

One more example can be taken from the agricultural income policy of Japan. According to the Agricultural Basic Law enacted in 1961, the government started to support the producers' rice price to maintain farm income at the level comparable with that for industrial workers. Farmers were satisfied with this price/income policy, but the consequence was that (1) the rice price soared up to a level four times higher than the international standard, (2) production was encouraged so much as to bring about a surplus of rice, and (3) financial burdens due to price support had to be borne by taxpayers.

5.2. Basic direction of agricultural policies in the 1980s

Agricultural problems to be solved at the beginning of the 1980s were to raise productivity and to eliminate the rice surplus. Considerations should be taken for further industrialization of the Japanese economy, changing eating habits of Japanese people, aging farm workers, numerous small sized farms, trends of trade liberalization, and strong urgency for food security.

The Agricultural Policy Council as an advisory organ to the Prime Minister was asked to analyze Japanese agriculture and factors surrounding it. In October 1980, the Council submitted the report entitled "Basic Direction of Agricultural Policies in the 1980s". It consists of seven chapters as follows:

(1) Development of the Japanese diet,
(2) Food security,
(3) Development prospect of the agricultural production,
(4) Agricultural price policies,
(5) Improvement of agricultural structure,
(6) Promotion of rural community development, and
(7) Measures for food processing industries and consumers.

It is proposed in the report that the Government should review minimum nutritional requirements of the nation, measures to ensure stable food imports, appropriate size of food reserves, and desirable pattern of agricultural production - all in preparation for possible embargo of food supply from abroad. Production should be reduced for those products for which demand is decreasing and promoted for those with increasing demand. Price policy should play the role of keeping demand and supply in balance. Productivity should be raised by enlarging farm size, promoting technological progress and introducing highly effective large machines.

The report is characterized by the idea that food supply should be secured by maintaining domestic production as far as possible rather than by depending more on food imports.

5.3. Basic direction of agricultural policies towards the 21st century

Agricultural development is to be harmonized with other industrial developments. Trade surplus accumulated by exporting manufactures has entailed trade liberalization including agricultural products. The requirement for Japan to carry out cooperative economic policies is growing more urgent in the world economy. The Agricultural Policy Council recognized these recent changing situations and submitted another report entitled "Basic Direction of Agricultural Policies Toward the 21st Century" in November 1986. In the report, attention was paid to strengthening the Japanese agricultural structure, diminishing the differentials between domestic and international prices for agricultural products, and reconsideration of protectionism in agricultural policies[7].

Concerning the demand and supply relation, the report is based on the recognition that the production capacity of the world is not fully utilized for the time being with respect to grains and other main agricultural products, but that uncertain factors about food supply still exist for the medium and long term period. Accordingly, it is ever necessary to make the most of national agricultural resources, to raise productivity and to maintain the production capacity of domestic foods. However, food provisions should be made at reasonable prices for consumers, domestic prices should be reduced through raising productivity and increasing imports of cheaper agricultural commodities to lower the food price index. In this sense it can be said that, in the new report, more stress would be put on the balance of domestic production and import of foods.

Judging from actual measures implemented since 1986, the most remarkable policy change was that the producers' rice price was cut down both in 1987 and 1988 for the first time since 1956 with an aim to recover the balance between demand for and supply of rice. This policy was disturbed in 1989 at the time of the general election for

---

7) Cf. Agricultural Policy Council 1981, pp. 1-3.

the House of Councillors, and the price cut for the year 1989 was postponed to the next year. Another remarkable measure was taken to open the market for oranges and beef after long and laborious negotiations with the United States, and import liberalization for these two items is scheduled to start in 1992 and 1991 respectively. Both policy changes imply that the protectionism in agricultural policies is going to be replaced gradually by the price mechanism as the free market principle.

6. Concluding remarks

It is often said that Japanese manufacturing is strongly competitive because MITI adopted an all-purpose industrial policy to foster a number of manufacturing industries. The name "Japan Inc." resulted from this fact. It is quite natural to ask what secrets there should have been in the successful results of the industrial policy of Japan. Prof. *Shinohara* points out three favorable factors[8]. The first one was the exchange rate of 360 yen against one US dollar at the time of rapid economic growth, when exports from Japan expanded very much with this exchange rate. The second one was the population size of more than 100 million, which made it possible for the domestic market to expand to the extent that mass production was realized and production costs were reduced. This factor is lacking in today's Asian NIEs. The third factor was the highly educated labor force, which enabled Japanese enterprises to introduce advanced technologies from abroad in the 1950s and 1960s. This activated investments in plant and equipment in which new technological innovations were embodied. It might be possible to add some other factors, but it would not be easy to find a necessity in the combination of these three factors.

One should note that Japanese enterprises were not always willing to follow the industrial policy pushed by MITI. There must have been expectations on the part of enterprises that benefits would be larger than costs when they cooperated with MITI. This attitude may have materialized the imagination of "Japan Inc.".

---

8) See *Shinohara* 1976, pp. 324-329.

References

Agricultural Policy Council: 80 nendai no nousei no kihon houkou (Basic Direction of Agricultural Policies in the 1980s), Tokyo (Souzou Shobo) 1981

Agricultural Policy Council, 21 seiki e muketeno nousei no kihon houkou (Basic Direction of Agricultural Policies Toward the 21st Century), Tokyo (Souzou Shobo) 1986

Economic Planning Agency, Economic Survey of Japan 1987-1988, Tokyo 1988

Economic Planning Agency, Economic Survey of Japan 1988-1989, Tokyo 1989

Komiya, R. (ed.), Nippon no sangyo seisaku (Industrial Policy of Japan), Tokyo (University of Tokyo Press) 1984

Konosu, K., What Will Be the Agricultural Policies of Japan in 1980s, Tokyo (Japan FAO Association) 1982

The Ministry of International Trade and Industry, Tsusho Hakusho (Annual Report of International Trade and Industry of Japan), Tokyo, yearly from 1986 to 1989

Morita, A., Made in Japan - Akio Morita and Sony, New York (E. P. Dutton) 1986

Reischauer, E. O., The Japanese, Cambridge (Harvard University Press) 1977

Shinohara, M., Sangyo kozo ron (On Industrial Structure), Tokyo (Chikuma Shobo) 1976

The Abandonment of the Gold Standard and Foreign Exchange / Tariff Policy - The Economic Lessons of the Great Depression in the Case of Japan -

Masanao Itoh

1. Preface

As it is well known, the Great Depression in the 1930s took place all over the world with unprecedented scale, depth and length. Under the Depression, the main countries one after another abandoned the gold standard and began to implement the managed currency system. At the same time, they adopted high protective or preferential tariffs and aimed to ensure closed market areas. Then, they rapidly progressed towards blocism for their individual escape from the economic crisis. The international gold standard system, which had been reconstructed in the 1920s, and the co-ordinating or adjusting mechanism of the world economy by this system were finally destroyed in the 1930s.

This process was immensely different in each country because of the difference of each position or performance in the world economy. This paper aims to investigate this process concerning the case of Japan. The problems are as follows: 1. How was the impact of the Great Depression on Japan, and why could Japan escape from the economic crisis so fast? 2. When and how did Japan abandon the gold standard, and what system was adopted for foreign exchange control? 3. What were the characteristics of economic policy after the abandonment of the gold standard, and what measures were taken for establishing a bloc economy?

2. The impact of the economic crisis (1930-31) in Japan

The economic crisis of 1930-31 was the deepest and biggest crisis in pre-war Japanese history. Table 1 shows that from 1929 to 1930, within only one year, capital investment in industry was halved and import and export levels also decreased by 30 %. Other indexes are much the same, on the whole. Yet compared with the other main countries, this crisis in Japan was relatively not so severe or violent. According to Figure 1, wholesale prices were falling till about 1933 in all countries except Japan, and their recovery was very slow. But only in Japan these prices began to rise again in 1932. The levels of GNP both in the U.S. and the U.K. were also reduced and did not turn back to their 1929's levels till 1934 (U.S.) and 1937 (U.K.).

In contrast with the indexes mentioned above, the trend of the wage contract cash earnings was different. Only in Japan they had been falling during the first half of the 1930s. From this point, we can suppose that Japan succeeded in wage control. Why did the wage deflation continue? Perhaps there were two factors; the influence of the crisis, and the structural change in industry. As a result of the crisis, many skilled laborers were left unemployed as redundant laborers. Due to the structural change in industry, young laborers were preferred. Their wage levels were, of course, cheaper than those of the elder and the senior, and many of them were supplied from rural districts. The period that labor supply became tight was about 1935 or 1936.

According to these facts, we can understand that this crisis in Japan had some characteristics different from the other countries.

1) Japan recovered so rapidly from the crisis.

2) Under the crisis, Japan kept the GNP in real terms at the level before the crisis.

3) The price falling ratio and the trade reducing ratio were higher than those of the other countries.

Additionally, we have to indicate the important economic or political affairs which occured before this crisis. Firstly, a financial crisis had taken place in 1927. At that time, the Bank of Taiwan and the Bank of Chosen, both of which had been governmental special banks and colonial central banks of Japan, went bankrupt. And many local small banks, over 30, also fell into bankruptcy. But when the crisis in 1930-31 occurred two years later, it did not involve a financial crisis. This is a strong contrast to the crises in Europe under the Great Depression.

Secondly, the return to the gold standard was carried out in 1930, although this was a little too late. Because of capital flight, much gold (= specie) flowed overseas. Table 2 shows the value of specie conversion in the period from 1930 to 1931 when Japan was still under the gold standard system. During this time, she lost over ¥ 700 thousand specie. Foreign banks and Japanese big banks converted many yen into specie directly or indirectly, and they bought dollar or sterling with these specie. The Yokohama Specie Bank, a governmental special bank and one of the big 3 foreign exchange banks in the world, made a great effort to keep the gold standard and to control the foreign exchange market under the conduct of the Government. Therefore, the Y.S.B. sold dollars unconditionally and unlimitedly as shown in Table 3. Half of those dollars were bought by foreign banks, and the others were bought by Japanese big banks and enterprises. But with this intervention, that is, the struggle for keeping the gold standard, the Japanese Government, the Bank of Japan and the Y.S.B. could not win. This failure occured because the Manchurian Incident (War) had arisen by the hand of the Japanese Army, and 3 days after the outbreak of this incident, the U.K. and the Sterling Area abandoned the gold standard. So the buyers of dollars strongly expected that Japan had to be forced to abandon the gold standard anyway. At the final phase of this process, the BOJ's official rate had been raised twice and that rate restrained not only foreign exchange demand for speculation but also for genuine purposes. The buyers' power, however, was not weakened. On Dec. 13, 1931, the Cabinet changed, and on the same day, the gold standard was abandoned. After this time, Japan turned to economic recovery at once.

3. Rapid recovery from the crisis

As we already pointed out, though in many countries of the world the condition of depression continued, Japan could escape from the crisis very quickly, just as Germany. The main force that led the economic condition to recovery was a rapid increase in industrial production. In the course of this recovery, metal, machinery and chemical industries took a central place among the composition of industry.

As shown in Table 4, the lowest point of total production was in 1931, and from 1932 all industries recovered. The increasing level of heavy industries, i.e., metals, machinery and chemicals, was also very strong. In the 1920s, their total value of products rose from 20 % to 30 % of that of all industrial products. But in the 1930s, their total value took up about 40 % or 50 %.

This increase of industrial production was brought about from three directions:

1) Armament demand by arsenals and private weapon enterprises; during the first half of the 1930s, Japanese Government had paid over ¥ 1000 million for extraordinary military expenses. Adding the military expenses in the general account to these, the total expenses reached about ¥ 800 million a year average. Then, there were also expenses for the expansion of armament and the Manchurian Incident. Therefore, the production level of army arsenals rose from 1932 (cf. Table 5).

2) Exports: Exports increased in two directions. One was towards underdeveloped countries (mainly South-East Asia), and main export goods were textiles. The other was towards Japanese colonies and half-colonies (mainly Manchuria and Korea), and here main export goods were metals, machinery and chemicals (cf. Table 6-1, Table 6-2).

Until the 1920s, Japan had large trade deficits which amounted to over ¥ 200 million a year on average. Yet owing to the increasing exports, though imports also were increasing, the trade balance became balanced. Consequently, this expansion of trade raised the industrial production at the early time of recovery.

3) Domestic demand: An increase of private investment in plant and equipment, and construction occured. Yet one must realize that before 1930, the textile industry took the central place in industry. Furthermore, the level of heavy industry , for example, the scale of enterprises or their technological levels, etc., were much lower than those in the U.S. or Europe. Therefore, if economic circumstances were adjusted or arranged, investment in heavy industries had to be increased rapidly. Conditions which made this possible were given by economic policies.

4. The effect of economic policies on the recovery

4.1. Foreign exchange policy

After the embargo of the gold standard, the yen exchange rate had depreciated falling rapidly, and it was then controlled and stabilized at the low level. The yen rate had decreased over 30 % during only two weeks, and the falling trend continued till the end of 1932 as shown in Figure 2 and Figure 3. The yen/dollar rate had fallen below the purchasing power parity. Mainly by this effect, Japanese exports increased. Therefore, the foreign exchange policy was a useful instrument for correcting the trade imbalance of Japan.

This policy was similar to those of the U.S. or the U.K. in appearance, but its substance or intention was equivalent to that of Germany. The U.S. and the U.K. also took undervaluating policies of exchange rates, and in this respect Japan was similar to them. Yet these countries had much foreign money for exchange controls. Japan had lost such money through the crisis and therefore could not implement this policy positively. Each of them had acted under the market mechanism, while Japan only used legal control. Japan enacted a law for slowing down capital flight in 1932, and then enacted a law for foreign exchange controls in 1933. By these laws, she almost could control capital transfers both in the short and long term. It was this point where Japan was similar to Germany. But Germany also was different from Japan in the following aspects.

Firstly, the level of productive force and productivity in Japan was much lower than in Germany. Japan, however, owed no war-debt and indemnity. Therefore, though Germany had to keep her exchange parity, Japan did not need to do so. Japanese exchange control was not so strong at this point.

Secondly, the effect by the exchange rate was relatively retained for a long time. As shown in Figure 2, the decreasing rate of the yen was much larger than those of the price level of tradable goods and domestic goods. Moreover, when we compare the price level of export with that of import goods, the rate of increase of the former was smaller than that of the latter. The reflection of this exchange rate decrease lagged very much.

4.2. Tariff policy

In June 1932, the specific tariff was raised substantially (about 35 %). This meant the protection of industries, especially metals and machinery. By this measure, Japanese heavy industries barely could supply the domestic market. For example, the tariff on pig iron was raised nearly four times and on steel one and half times as high as those in 1932 (cf. Table 7). As a result of this, the prices of domestic products became cheaper than import prices.

4.3. Financial/monetary policy

Furthermore, in this period, the maximum limit of the Bank of Japan note issued had been expanded from ¥ 120 million to ¥ 1 billion. Government expenditure, including the war expenditure, increased rapidly because of the way that the BOJ undertook the deficit-covering government bond. Additionally, the official discount rate and principal interest rates were reduced for political reasons. We could consider this policy as a "pre-*Keynes*ian" policy, or at least an unintended demand management policy.

In conclusion, Japan succeeded in rapid economic recovery by adopting these policies. However, this success did not mean a radical or fundamental solution. Concerning foreign relations, her over- expansion of export brought about a hard conflict with the U.K. and others, since the main market for textile export still consisted of the Sterling Area countries. Moreover, classifying according to regions, the balance of payment revealed a negative tendency. Japan could again trade surplus only from the yen bloc area. Outside this area, Japan could not get any foreign money, e.g. dollar or pound sterling (cf. Table 8). Furthermore, Japan could not get so much material for heavy industries from the yen bloc area, so that import goods from other areas gradually increased. And this had made Japan increasingly lose foreign money. Regarding the domestic economy, Japan reached the full employment condition of labor and equipment by about 1936. As a result, labor supply became very tight, and at the same time a galloping inflation began. The shortage of material in heavy industries became striking. To escape from this bottle-neck, Japan had again chosen imperialistic aggression. In 1937, the war between Japan and China began.

References

Arndt, H., The Economic Lessons of the Nineteen-Thirties, First Edition, London (Frank Cass & Co. Ltd.) 1944

The Bank of Japan, Nihon Ginko 100 Nenshi (The History of the Bank of Japan in 100 Years), Tokyo (Nihon Shin-yo Chosa Co. Ltd.) 1986

The Bank of Tokyo, Yokohama Shokin Ginko Zenshi (The History of the Yokohama Specie Bank in the Pre-War's Period), Tokyo (Toyo Keizai Shinposha) 1980

Drummond, I., The Gold Standard and the International Monetary System 1900-1939, Houndmills (Macmillan Education Ltd.) 1987

Hashimoto, J., Daikyokoki no Nihon Shihonshugi (Japanese Capitalism during the Great Depression), Tokyo (Tokyo University Press) 1984

Kindleberger, C., The World in Depression 1929-1939, Berkeley (University of California Press) 1973

Ministry of Army, The History of Army Arsenals, unpublished, no year

Ministry of Commerce and Industry, Seitetsugyo Sanko Shiryo (Annual Report of Iron and Steel Industries), Tokyo, no year

Ministry of Finance, Kinyu Jiko Sankosho (Annual Report of the Finances), Tokyo, no year

Ministry of Finance, Showa Zaiseishi, Vol. 13 (The Financial History of Japan 1926-1945), Tokyo (Toyo Keizai Shinposha) 1963

Sayers, R., The Bank of England 1891-1944, London (Cambridge University Press) 1976

Shinohara, M., Long Term Economic Statistics, Vol. 10, Tokyo (Toyo Keizai Shinposha) 1972

Yamazawa, I./*Yamamoto*, Y., Long Term Economic Statistics, Vol. 14, Tokyo (Toyo Keizai Shinposha) 1979

Figure 1: International Comparison of Main Economic Indexes

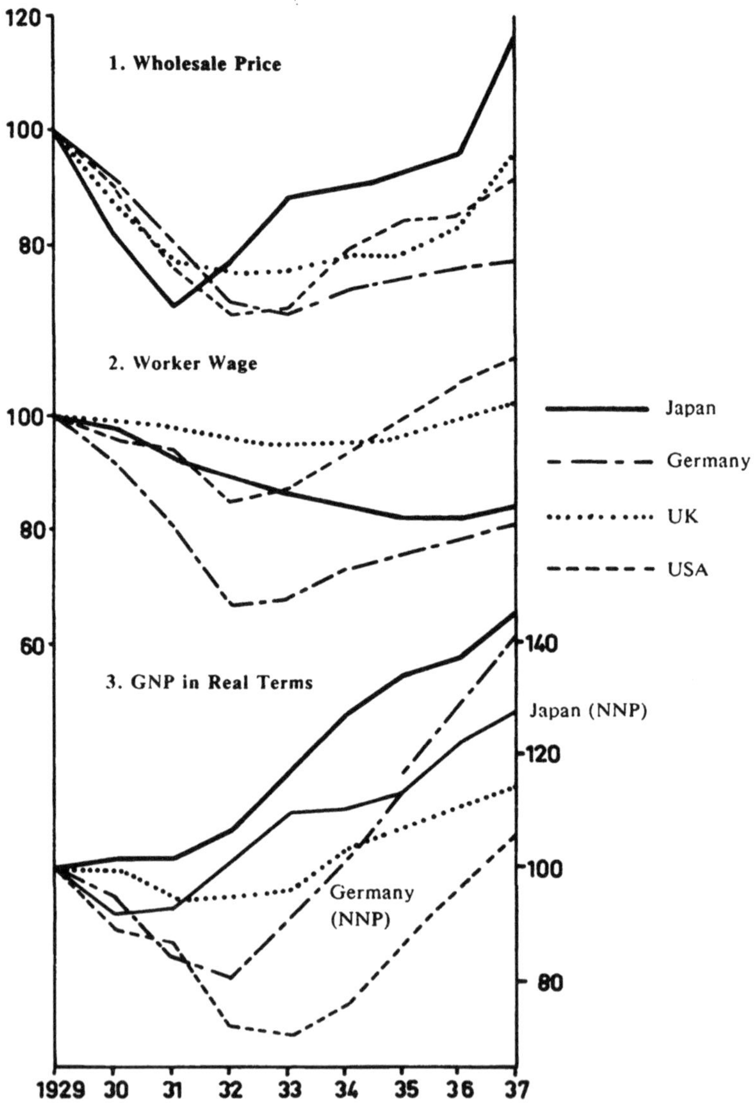

Source: Hashimoto 1984

Figure 2: Foreign Exchange, Prices, Currency

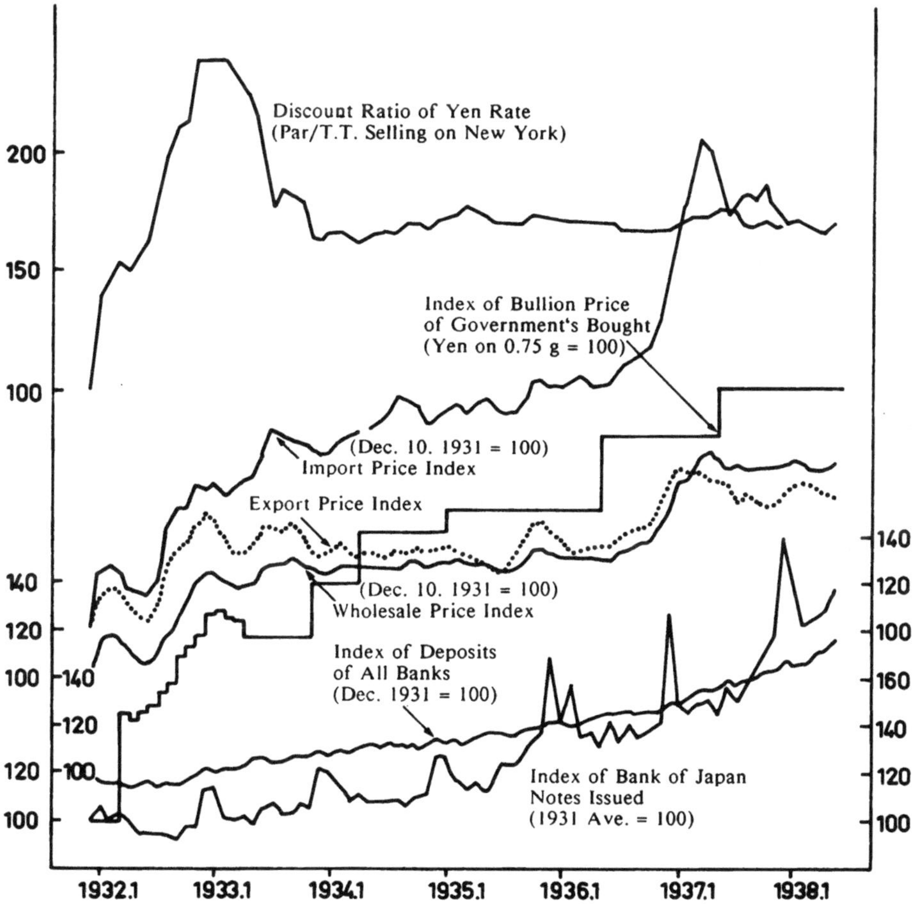

Source: MOF "Kinyu Jiko Sankosho", etc.

Figure 3: Foreign Exchange Rates

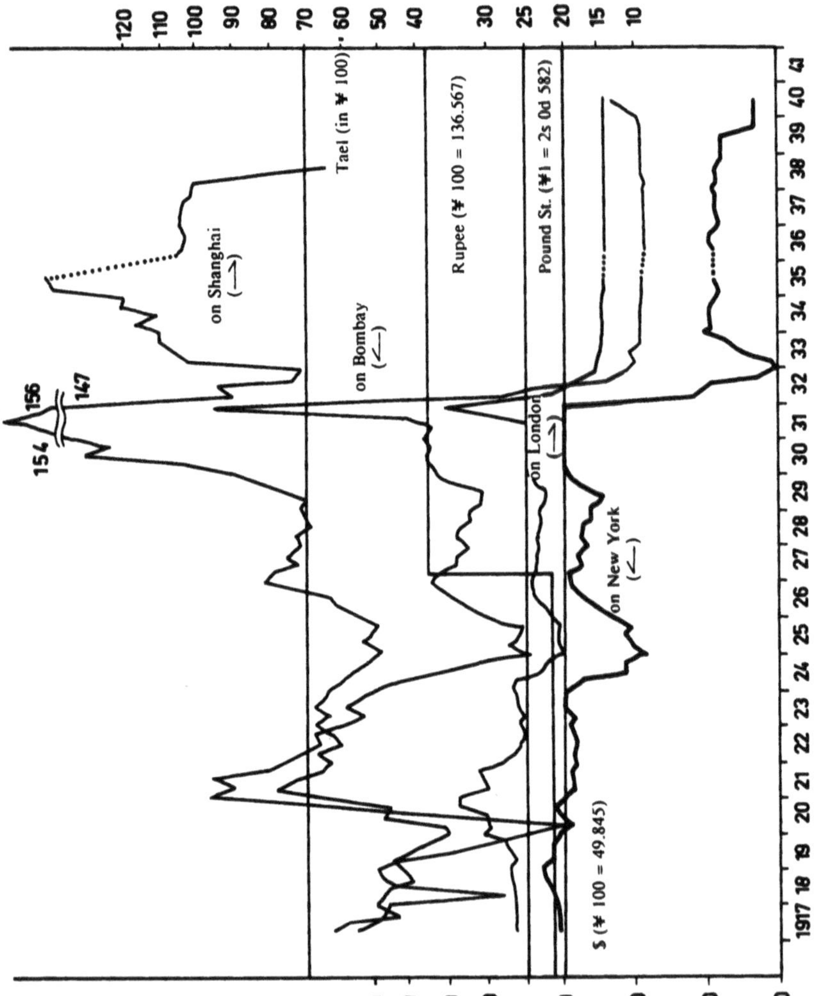

Source: MOF

Table 1: Main Indexes of 1930 - 31 Crisis

	1926	1927	1928	1929	1930	1931	1932	1933
1. Consumer Price	108.1	106.5	102.4	100.0	89.8	79.5	80.4	82.9
2. Stock Price	146.1	134.0	125.1	100.0	61.7	62.7	78.6	113.1
3. Capital Investment by Industry	159.1	146.1	139.8	(1,041)* 100.0	43.8	53.5	42.1	109.0
4. Profit Ratio (Paid-in Capital)	9.8	9.8	8.8	8.3	6.6	5.0	5.8	7.9
5. Railways Traffic	96.4	101.8	103.8	(85,264)+ 100.0	83.1	78.1	79.0	91.5
6. Number of Workers Employed	100.0	98.4	90.4	91.1	82.2	74.4	74.7	81.9
7. Real Cash Earnings (Male)	100.0	102.1	105.3	103.9	98.7	90.7	88.1	89.2
8. Real Cash Earnings (Female)	100.0	99.4	99.8	96.4	87.4	77.4	70.9	68.6
9. Number of Labor Disputes	1,260	1,202	1,013	1,408	2,284	2,415	2,159	1,859
10. Number of Peasant Disputes	2,751	2,052	1,866	2,424	2,478	3,419	3,414	4,000
11. Bank of Japan Notes Issued	95.6	102.5	106.0	(1,641)* 100.0	87.5	81.0	86.9	94.1
12. Deposits of Ordinary Banks	98.8	97.1	100.4	(9,292)* 100.0	94.0	89.0	89.5	94.9
13. Lendings of Ordinary Banks	127.2	112.9	104.1	(7,246)* 100.0	94.1	91.0	87.5	84.0
14. Value of Checks and Bills Clearances	140.2	98.8	108.1	(63,795)* 100.0	81.2	72.7	83.1	105.3
15. Discounts of Commercial Bills	2.40 - 1.95	2.10 - 1.50	1.90 - 1.35	1.90 - 1.30	1.90 - 1.30	2.00 - 1.40	1.80 - 1.15	1.70 - 1.20
16. Call Rates	2.10 - 1.55	1.60 - 0.70	1.70 - 0.60	1.50 - 0.65	1.50 - 0.70	2.50 - 1.60	1.05 - 0.60	1.10 - 0.60
17. Value of Imports	95.2	92.7	91.8	(2,148)* 100.0	68.4	53.4	65.6	86.6
18. Value of Exports	107.3	98.3	99.1	(2,216)* 100.0	69.8	55.8	64.6	86.5

Source: MOF, MITI, BOJ, TEM, etc. * (million ¥) + (thousand tons)

Table 2: **Specie Conversion, Flight out of Gold**

(thousands Yen)

		Foreign Banks	Y. S. B.	Other Japanese Banks	Total	Flight out of Gold
1930	1	42,160	–	6,063	48,223	44,800
	2	25,800	–	39,000	64,800	84,995
	3	7,800	–	27,000	34,800	46,101
	4	27,900	–	–	27,900	23,399
	5	19,800	–	–	19,800	19,905
	6	4,000	–	–	4,000	3,481
	7	–	–	–	–	△2,842
Total		127,400	–	72,063	199,463	219,839
	8	13,800	–	–	13,800	18,972
	9	2,200	5,000	–	7,200	8,348
	10	–	40,000	–	40,000	39,457
	11	–	15,000	–	15,000	14,089
	12	–	–	–	–	△1,121
1931	1	1,500	–	–	1,500	390
	2	1,200	–	1,000	2,200	168
	3	5,300	–	1,000	6,300	4,300
	4	–	–	–	–	2,327
	5	800	–	–	800	283
	6	2,500	–	–	2,500	1,296
	7	800	45,000	–	45,800	29,570
	8	–	20,000	–	20,000	18,595
Total		28,100	125,000	2,000	155,100	136,674
	9	–	–	–	–	△236
	10	–	135,000	–	135,000	135,123
	11	–	146,500	–	146,500	146,321
	12	–	72,500	–	72,500	52,500
Total		–	354,000	–	354,000	333,708
Total		155,560	479,000	74,063	708,623	690,224

Source: BOJ

Table 3: Value of Foreign Exchange Selling by Y.S.B. for Foreign Exchange Control

(Sep. 21, 1931 - Nov. 3, 1931)

	Dollars	in thousand Yen
National City Bank of N. Y.	37,005,000	74,010
Mitsui Bank	21,350,000	42,700
Mitsui & Co.	14,227,700	28,455
Sumitomo Bank	12,350,000	24,700
Mitsubishi Bank	8,700,000	17,400
Bank of Chosen	6,140,000	12,280
Hongkong & Shanghai Bank	4,800,000	9,600
Toyo Menka Ltd. (Cotton)	4,443,750	8,888
Nomura Security	3,670,000	7,340
Mitsui Trust Co.	3,500,000	7,000
Charterd Bank of I. A. & C.	3,100,000	6,200
Kawasaki Asihyak Bank	2,900,000	5,800
Nederlandsh-Indische Handelsbank	2,490,000	4,980
J. S. Trading Co.	2,358,000	4,716
Tokyo Electric Co.	2,000,000	4,000
Bank of Taiwan	1,800,000	3,600
Netherlands Trading Society	1,790,000	3,580
Daido Electric Co.	1,470,000	2,940

Source: BOJ

Table 4: Value of Production in the Manufacturing Industry

(Current Prices, million Yen, %)

	Heavy Industries				Other Industries			Total	Self-Sustaining Ratio		
	Chemicals	Metals	Machinery	Total	Food	Textiles	Total	(with others)	Che-micals	Metals	Machi-nery
1914	312(12)	128(5)	269(11)	709(28)	815(32)	830(32)	1,645(64)	2,561(100)	85	85	90
19	1,092(10)	839(7)	1,472(13)	3,403(31)	2,111(19)	4,599(41)	6,710(60)	11,159(100)	87	78	95
23	911(10)	525(6)	671(7)	2,107(23)	2,379(26)	3,399(38)	5,778(64)	9,039(100)	83	77	83
26	1,059(11)	679(7)	839(8)	2,577(26)	2,597(26)	3,663(36)	6,260(62)	10,046(100)	84	80	87
27	1,089(11)	694(7)	938(9)	2,721(27)	2,544(26)	3,485(35)	6,029(60)	9,975(100)	87	83	91
28	1,189(11)	819(8)	969(9)	2,960(28)	2,657(25)	3,689(35)	6,346(60)	10,536(100)	88	83	90
29	1,308(12)	927(9)	1,008(9)	3,243(30)	2,482(23)	3,773(35)	6,255(58)	10,744(100)	89	86	90
30	1,134(13)	767(9)	994(11)	2,895(33)	2,206(25)	2,709(31)	4,915(56)	8,838(100)	93	94	95
31	997(13)	611(8)	694(9)	2,302(29)	2,010(26)	2,562(33)	4,572(58)	7,877(100)	92	97	97
32	1,168(13)	838(10)	849(10)	2,854(32)	1,987(23)	2,859(32)	4,846(55)	8,814(100)	94	96	97
33	1,532(14)	1,267(11)	1,178(11)	3,976(36)	2,259(20)	3,628(32)	5,887(53)	11,166(100)	97	94	100
34	1,773(14)	1,563(12)	1,731(13)	5,066(39)	2,346(18)	4,098(31)	6,444(50)	13,015(100)	99	93	102
35	2,149(14)	1,921(13)	2,446(16)	6,515(44)	2,461(16)	4,356(29)	6,817(46)	14,968(100)	100	93	103
36	2,484(15)	2,245(14)	2,599(16)	7,327(45)	2,590(16)	4,562(28)	7,152(44)	16,280(100)	100	96	105
37	3,385(16)	3,533(17)	3,521(17)	10,437(50)	2,739(13)	5,604(27)	8,347(40)	21,072(100)	97	88	103

Source: Shinohara "Long Term Economic Statistics", vol. 10

Table 5: Value and Volume of Production in Army Arsenal

	Total (10 thousand Yen)			Volume of Production of Main Weapons (No.)			Number of Employees
		Weapons Production	Weapons Holding	Rifles	Machine-guns	Artilleries	
1926	n.a.	n.a.	5,450	3,038	1,174	111	10,818
27	3,694	1,900	3,920	1,525	1,195	106	10,948
28	3,570	1,730	3,710	6,820	1,054	137	11,090
29	3,650	1,770	3,748	3,836	788	97	10,898
30	3,985	2,035	4,029	3,942	971	116	11,352
31	3,737	1,950	4,467	3,613	541	66	12,702
32	6,198	3,861	6,794	1,060	1,069	34	17,537
33	8,620	5,610	9,746	2,250	6,100	n.a.	21,006
34	9,590	6,050	10,919	2,780	4,300	n.a.	22,145
35	9,420	6,180	11,460	6,800	3,000	n.a.	21,680
36	9,540	5,930	10,815	25,300	2,400	n.a.	24,768
37	26,680	17,050	47,140	42,754	2,280	44	88,124

Source: Ministry of Army's Historical Materials

Table 6.1: Exports and Imports Classified by Regions

(Current Price, million Yen, %)

Exports	1931	1934	1937	1931→1934	1934→1937
I. Advanced Areas	543.0 (36.7)	635.4 (22.8)	1,015.9 (24.2)	92.4	380.5
North America	438.9	407.6	659.6	△31.3	252.0
Europe	104.1	227.8	356.2	123.7	232.6
II. Underdeveloped Areas	380.7 (25.8)	1,016.4 (36.4)	1,350.2 (32.2)	635.7	333.8
Southeast Asia	109.5	289.2	386.7	179.7	97.5
Other Asia	122.5	315.2	394.8	192.7	79.6
Others	26.6	79.9	106.5	53.3	26.6
III. Colony and Half-Colony	555.9 (37.6)	1,136.8 (40.8)	1,822.6 (43.5)	580.9	685.8
Korea	217.8	439.6	753.4	221.8	313.8
Taiwan	114.8	177.0	277.9	62.2	100.9
Manchuria	79.4	403.1	612.0	323.7	208.9
China	143.9	117.1	179.3	26.8	62.2
Total	1,479.6 (100.0)	2,788.6 (100.0)	4,188.7 (100.0)	1,309.0	1,400.1
Imports	**1931**	**1934**	**1937**	**1931→1934**	**1934→1937**
I. Advanced Areas	577.7 (34.7)	1,119.1 (38.1)	1,878.1 (39.4)	541.4	759.0
North America	378.0	823.5	1,374.1	445.5	550.6
Europe	199.7	295.6	504.0	95.9	208.4
II. Underdeveloped Areas	391.8 (23.5)	819.7 (27.9)	1,467.2 (30.8)	427.9	647.5
Southeast Asia	93.3	165.1	373.7	71.8	208.6
Other Asia	133.5	301.7	474.3	168.2	172.6
Others	117.5	214.3	222.1	96.8	6.8
III. Colony and Half-Colony	686.2 (41.2)	998.2 (34.0)	1,420.6 (29.8)	312.0	422.4
Korea	249.0	407.7	572.4	158.7	164.7
Taiwan	201.4	279.4	410.3	78.0	130.9
Manchuria	132.1	191.5	294.3	59.4	102.8
China	103.7	119.6	143.6	15.9	24.0
Total	1,665.1 (100.0)	2,937.0 (100.0)	4,765.9 (100.0)	1,271.9	1,828.9

Source: Yamazawa & Yamamoto "Long Term Economic Statistics", vol. 14

Table 6.2: Exports and Imports Classified by Industry (Current Price, million Yen)

Exports	1931	1934	1937	1931→34	1934→37
Primary Products	114.5	175.5	262.1	61.0	86.6
Food and Textiles	1,060.1	1,897.0	2,677.1	836.9	780.1
Raw Silk Yarn	356.9	287.7	409.1	△69.2	121.4
Cotton Fabrics	229.7	553.8	627.0	324.1	73.2
Artificial Silk	159.1	391.9	598.8	232.8	207.7
Heavy Industrial Products	251.5	640.9	1,154.6	389.4	513.7
Machinery	61.5	186.9	363.3	125.4	176.4
Metal Products	75.0	203.3	384.2	128.3	180.9
Chemicals	115.0	250.7	407.1	135.7	156.4
Total	1,426.1	2,713.4	4,093.8	1,287.3	1,380.4
Imports	**1931**	**1934**	**1937**	**1931→34**	**1934→37**
Primary Products	985.1	1,896.4	2,708.8	911.3	812.4
Crude Foodstuff	335.3	538.8	662.4	183.0	124.1
Textile Materials	401.9	956.2	1,202.6	554.3	246.4
Metal Products and Materials	139.2	218.0	519.3	78.8	301.3
Food and Textiles	309.6	307.4	408.3	△2.2	100.9
Heavy Industrial Products	367.3	734.0	1,595.3	366.7	861.3
Machinery	83.0	146.2	248.8	13.2	102.6
Metal Products	92.1	315.4	853.3	223.3	537.9
Chemicals	192.2	272.4	493.2	80.2	220.8
Total	1,662.0	2,937.8	4,712.4	1,275.8	1,774.6

Source: Yamazawa & Yamamoto "Long Term Economic Statistics", vol. 14

Table 7: Import Tariffs on Iron and Steel

(Yen on ton)

	before 1932	Plan of Syokosyo (1931. 11. 20)	Changed Rate in 1932
Pig Iron	1.67	10	6
Steel Bars and Rods	18.33	25	24.66
Rail	15.83	25	21.33
Sheet & 3 ~ 0.7 mm	23.33	30	31.50
Plates 3 mm	18.33	25	24.66
0.7 mm	32.5	35	43.83
Wire	18%	25	21.66

Source: MOCI

Table 8: Balance of Payments Classified by Regions

(million Yen)

	Trade Balance		Invisible Trade Balance		Overall Balance		c. f. Investment on Manchuria
	Yen Bloc Area	Others	Yen Bloc Area	Others	Yen Bloc Area	Others	
1932	0	Δ67	2		Δ65		97
33	121	Δ205	89		5		161
34	199	Δ345	Δ39		Δ185		252
35	197	Δ214	Δ193		Δ210		382
36	221	Δ349	Δ244	206	Δ22	Δ142	264
37	326	Δ963	Δ666	80	Δ340	Δ883	453
38	597	Δ537	Δ942	103	Δ345	Δ434	525

Source: Yamazawa & Yamamoto "Long Term Economic Statistics", vol. 14

Real and Monetary Shocks in a Dynamic Two-Country Model

Ryuhei Okumura

1. Introduction

It is generally said that the flexible exchange rate regime can insulate an economy from foreign monetary shocks, but not from foreign real shocks (i.e., *Hamada* 1985, p. 97). In other words, monetary shocks change only the exchange rate, leaving other real variables, such as the terms of trade and the real interest rate, uninfluenced. On the other hand, real shocks do change real variables.

This view has yet to be investigated fully in an intertemporal optimizing model of the world economy. The recent works by *Frankel* and *Rasin* (1985, 1986), which are properly based on the intertemporal optimizing behavior of economic agents, analyze only real shocks (fiscal policies).

In this paper, we consider the effects of both real and monetary shocks. In the framework of a classical flexible price model, we specifically analyze the effects of an increase in the money growth rate and a reduction in government expenditure regarding world rates of interest, consumption and international indebtedness.

The features of our model are: (1) Every demand function is derived from an intertemporal utility maximization problem which is based on perfect foresight, (2) capital mobility between two countries is perfect, (3) the household's subjective rate of time preference is determined endogenously, (4) the household's utility depends on consumption and money holdings. In this sense, our model can be regarded as an extension of the model by *Obstfeld* (1981) to a two-country world.

However, since real interest rates are endogenous in our model, real and monetary shocks affect the utility levels of both countries. These results are different from *Obstfeld*'s results.

We can show that an increase in the money growth rate of one country reduces the real interest rate and decreases the utility levels of both countries; a reduction in government expenditure raises the real interest rate and increases the utility levels of both countries in a stationary state. Thus, neither real nor monetary shocks are neutral in this intertemporal optimizing model of the world economy.

The outline of the paper is as follows. Section 2 describes the general framework of the model and the intertemporal maximization problem of the representative household. Introducing the government budget constraint and the equilibrium condition of commodity and money markets, we close the model. In section 3, we solve the maximization problem and interpret its implication. Finally, we analyze the effects of real and monetary shocks under the condition of a stationary state.

2. The model

2. 1. The framework of the model

Consider a two-country world with flexible exchange rates. Each country produces the same composite goods at the full employment level. Identical households possess two kinds of assets: money and real bonds. It is assumed that households do not possess any of the other country's money. Bonds are denominated in terms of goods and real interest rates are flexible under perfect capital mobility. The real interest rates of the two countries will be equalized.

In order to depict the model more clearly, we have introduced the following notation:

c_t consumption of goods
m_t real money holdings
b_t real bond holdings
a_t real value of material wealth

Y	output (at full employment)
r_t	real interest rate
P_t	price of goods
π_t	inflation rate
M_t	nominal existing stock of money
E_t	nominal exchange rate
τ_t	net real transfer
g	real government spending
μ	money growth rate

where all variables are at time t. The asterisk (*) will be used to indicate the foreign country's variables.

2. 2. *Households*

Without loss of generality, we assume the number of households to be one.

We also assume that the household's instantaneous utility function is,

$$(1) \qquad u_t = U(c_t, m_t)$$

with the property that,

$$U_c > 0,\ U_{cc} < 0,\ U_m > 0,\ U_{mm} < 0,\ U_{cm} = 0,\ \lim_{c\to 0} U_c = \infty,\ \lim_{m\to 0} U_m = \infty.$$

The household is assumed to maximize the discounted sum of instantaneous utilities over an infinite time period,

$$(2) \qquad V = \int_0^\infty U(c_t, m_t) e^{-\Delta_t}\, dt$$

where discount factor Δ_t is the accumulated value of the positive instantaneous subjective discount rate at time s,

$$(3) \qquad \Delta_t = \int_0^t \delta_s\, ds$$

Following *Uzawa* (1968) and *Obstfeld* (1981), we suppose that δ_s is a function of utility at time s,

$$(4)\quad \delta_s = \delta(u_s)$$

with the property that,

$$\delta'(u_s)>0,\ \delta''(u_s)>0,\ \delta(u_s)-u_s\delta'(u_s)>0.$$

The first condition implies that an increase in utility at time s will increase the instantaneous discount rate for all future utilities after time s. The last condition assures that the discounted value of utility is an increasing function of utility in the stationary state.

The behavior of the household is subject to three constraints. First, total real material wealth must be allocated between real money holdings and real bond holdings in such manner that,

$$(5)\quad a_t = m_t + b_t.$$

Second, the real value of material wealth increases (decreases) when real saving is positive (negative). Real saving is the discrepancy between the real disposable income and real consumption. Real disposable income is defined as,

$$(6)\quad Y_t^d = Y + r_t b_t + \tau_t - \pi_t m_t.$$

Therefore, the flow constraint which governs asset accumulation can be written as,

$$(7)\quad \dot{a}_t = Y + r_t b_t + \tau_t - \pi_t m_t - c_t$$

$$= Y + r_t a_t + \tau_t - c_t - (r_t + \pi_t) m_t .$$

Finally, to exclude the possibility that the household borrows unbounded amounts in the perfect capital market, we impose the following intertemporal budget constraint,

$$(8)\quad \int_0^\infty [c_t + (r_t + \pi_t) m_t] e^{-R_t}\, dt$$

$$\leq a_0 + \int_0^\infty (Y + \tau_t) e^{-R_t}\, dt$$

where $R_t = \int_0^t r_s ds$.

The household's optimization problem is to find the paths

$\{c_t, m_t\}_{t=0}^{t=\infty}$ that maximize (2) subject to (5), (7), (8), given a_0.

2. 3. Government

We assume that the government levies taxes on and makes transfers to the household, and consumes composite goods. Net transfer payments and expenditure on goods are financed by money creation.

Also, we assume that the real government spending and the money growth rate are exogeneous policy parameters. The real net transfer is determined by the equation,

$$(9)\quad \tau_t = \mu m_t - g$$

We suppose $\mu + r_t > 0$, for all t. Without this assumption, we may not find a stationary state equilibrium. This means that the nominal interest rate is positive.

2. 4. Market equilibrium

Market equilibrium requires the following conditions at each time t:

Commodity Arbitrage Equation

(10) $P_t = E_t P_t^*$

Real Interest Rate Arbitrage Equation

(11) $r_t = r_t^*$

Commodity Market Clearing Condition

(12) $c_t + g + c_t^* + g^* = Y + Y^*$

Domestic Money Market Clearing Condition

(13) $m_t = M_t / P_t$

Foreign Money Market Clearing Condition

(14) $m_t^* = M_t^* / P_t^*$

These conditions are fairly standard, so an extra explanation is not necessary.

3. Analysis

3. 1. Solution of the utility maximization problem

Following *Uzawa* and *Obstfeld*, we can solve the optimization problem.

First, in order to simplify the problem, we change the time variables from t to "psychological time". Using the relationship,

$$(15)\quad d\Delta = \delta[U(c_t, m_t)]dt$$

we can rewrite the optimization problem as,

$$(16)\quad \text{Max} \int_0^\infty \frac{U(C, m)}{\delta[U(c, m)]} e^{-\Delta} d\Delta$$

$$(17)\quad \text{s.t.}\ \frac{da}{d\Delta} = \frac{Y+ra+\tau-c-(r+\pi)m}{\delta[U(c, m)]}$$

where the psychological time subscripts are omitted for simplicity.

Applying the Maximum Principle, we define the current-value *Hamilton*ian,

$$(18)\quad H = \frac{U(c, m)}{\delta[U(c, m)]} + \lambda \frac{[Y+ra+\tau-c-(r+\pi)m]}{\delta[U(c, m)]}$$

where λ is the co-state variable, in other words, the shadow price of material assets.

The necessary conditions require that c and m maximize the current-value *Hamilton*ian, and the co-state variable moves according to the differential equation,

$$(19)\quad \frac{d\lambda}{d\Delta} = \lambda \left(\frac{\delta - r}{\delta} \right)$$

Replacing the time variable Δ with the original time variable t, we obtain (20) from (19),

$$(20)\quad \dot{\lambda} = \frac{d\lambda}{d\Delta} \cdot \frac{d\Delta}{dt} = \lambda_t \{\delta[U(c_t, m_t)] - r_t\}$$

and the first order conditions of an interior maximum are reduced to the following equality:

$$(21)\quad U_m(c_t, m_t)/U_c(c_t, m_t) = r_t + \pi_t$$

This Equation implies that a rise in the nominal interest rate causes a substitution from real money holdings to consumption[1].

If the paths of price, real interest rate and real net transfer are given, Equations (20), (21), and (7) determine the variables time path

$$\{c_t, m_t\}_{t=0}^{t=\infty}.$$

For the foreign country, there is a similar result.

If we combine these household demand functions with the above-mentioned market equilibrium conditions, we will obtain the paths

[1] The intertemporal budget constraint (8) ensures the transversality conditions. See Appendix B in *Obstfeld* 1981.

of price, real interest rates and exchange rates. Since we assume perfect foresight, the expectations which the household relies on do not contradict the actual paths of price and real interest rate.

3. 2. The stationary state

We confine the analysis of real and monetary shocks to the stationary state, because of its manageability.

The stationary state

$$(\bar{c}, \bar{m}, \bar{c}^*, \bar{m}^*, \bar{r}, \bar{\pi}, \bar{\pi}^*)$$

must satisfy the following conditions:

$$(22) \quad U_m(\bar{c}, \bar{m})/U_c(\bar{c}, \bar{m}) = \bar{\pi} + \bar{r}$$

$$(23) \quad U_m^*(\bar{c}^*, \bar{m}^*)/U_c^*(\bar{c}^*, \bar{m}^*) = \bar{\pi}^* + \bar{r}$$

$$(24) \quad \delta[U(\bar{c}, \bar{m})] = \bar{r}$$

$$(25) \quad \delta^*[U^*(\bar{c}^*, \bar{m}^*)] = \bar{r}$$

$$(26) \quad \bar{\pi} = \mu$$

$$(27) \quad \bar{\pi}^* = \mu^*$$

$$(28) \quad \bar{c} + \bar{c}^* = y + y^*$$

where $y = Y - g$, $y^* = Y^* - g$.

The Equations: (26) and (27) are money market clearing conditions. In the stationary state, real money holdings will not change, so the inflation rate will be equal to the money growth rate. Using Equations (10), (26) and (27), we can show the rate of change in the exchange rate as,

$$(29)\quad \dot{E}/E = \bar{\pi} - \bar{\pi}^{*} = \mu - \mu^{*}$$

The Equations (24) and (25) correspond to the differential equations governing the movement of the co-state variables (i.e., Equation (20)).

The stationary state can be depicted in two diagrams. First, from Equations (24) and (25), we can see that the utility levels of both countries depend on the real interest rate solely. Figure 1 shows this.

Second, given the utility levels of both countries, we can determine the optimum combinations of consumption and real money holdings of both countries as in Figure 2. Where two indifference maps are combined in one diagram, point 0 and point 0* are the origins of domestic and foreign countries' indifference maps. The combination of consumption and real money holdings is determined by the condition that the marginal rate of substitution between them is equal to the nominal rate of interest in each country. For the arbitrary real interest rate, the sum $c+c^*$ may not be equal to the sum $y+y^*$. If $y+y^*$ exceeds $c+c^*$, the real interest rate must rise to encourage more consumption, according to assumption $\delta' > 0$. This rise in the real interest rate will cause the increase in the utility levels and consumption in both countries. This movement will continue until the goods market equilibrium condition (28) is established. The opposite will occur if $c+c^*$ exceeds $y+y^*$.

3. 3. Effects of real and monetary shocks

Now, we will analyze the effects of real and monetary disturbances in the stationary state.

Set $x(c, m) = U_m(c, m)/U_c(c, m)$.

The assumption of separability ($U_{cm} = 0$) assures result $x_c > 0$ and $x_m < 0$.[2]

After substituting Equations (26) and (27) into Equations (22) and (23), we differentiate the stationary state conditions to obtain the equations of change.

$$(30)\quad \begin{pmatrix} x_c & 0 & x_m & 0 & -1 \\ 0 & x_c^* & 0 & x_m^* & -1 \\ \delta' U_c & 0 & \delta' U_m & 0 & -1 \\ 0 & \delta^{*\prime} U_c^* & 0 & \delta^{*\prime} U_m^* & -1 \\ 1 & 1 & 0 & 0 & 0 \end{pmatrix} \begin{pmatrix} d\bar{c} \\ d\bar{c}^* \\ d\bar{m} \\ d\bar{m}^* \\ d\bar{r} \end{pmatrix} = \begin{pmatrix} d\mu \\ d\mu^* \\ 0 \\ 0 \\ dy+dy^* \end{pmatrix}$$

2) Because

$$x_c = (U_{cm}U_c - U_{cc}U_m)/U_c^2, \quad x_m = (U_{mm}U_c - U_{cm}U_m)/U_c^2$$

and $U_{cc}, U_{mm} < 0$.

Monetary shock: Suppose the domestic country increases the money growth rate. Solving Equation (30), we can obtain the following results[3]:

$$d\bar{c}/d\mu > 0, \quad d\bar{m}/d\mu < 0, \quad d\bar{c}^*/d\mu < 0,$$

$$d\bar{m}^*/d\mu \gtreqless 0 \text{ according as } \delta^{*\prime} U_c^* \gtreqless x_c^*$$

$$d\bar{r}/d\mu < 0, \quad |d\bar{r}/d\mu| < 1$$

The meaning of these results is explained by using Figure 3, and Figure 4. The increase of the money growth rate raises the inflation rate in the domestic country. If the real interest rate is held constant, the nominal interest rate will rise in the domestic country. By the substitution effect, real money holdings will decrease, and consumption will increase (A → B in Figure 3). In the goods market, excess demand rises; this requires a decrease in the real interest rate (B → C in Figure 3). In the foreign country, the inflation rate does not change, but the reduction in the real interest rate causes a decrease in the utility level and consumption (A → B in Figure 4). The increase in the money growth rate of the domestic country decreases the utility levels in both countries.

Furthermore, the magnitude of the reduction in the real interest rate is less than proportional. This means that the nominal interest rate also increases, but by less than the increase in the rate of inflation in the domestic country.

Summing up these results, the increase in the money growth rate raises the inflation rate and the nominal interest rate in the domestic country. However, this decreases the real interest rate, and reduces the utility levels of both countries[4]. As *Mundell* (1963) similarly

---

3) See Appendix 1 for the detailed formulas.

4) *Rodriguez* (1982) shows this result in a different two-country model. But he does not analyze a real shock.

states, "real conditions in the economy are altered by the purely monetary phenomenon"[5].

Real shock: We consider the effects of a reduction in domestic government expenditures as a real shock. This is equivalent to an exogenous increase in domestic output, because dy = dY - dg.

By solving Equation (30) with dy > 0, we can obtain the following results[6]:

$d\bar{c}/dy > 0, \; d\bar{m}/dy \gtreqless 0$ according to $\delta' U_c \lesseqgtr x_c$

$d\bar{c}^*/dy > 0, \; d\bar{m}^*/dy \gtreqless 0$ according to $\delta^{*\prime} U_c^* \lesseqgtr x_c^*$

$d\bar{r}/dy > 0$

Therefore, a reduction in domestic government expenditures raises the real interest rate and the utility levels of both countries in the stationary state.

The movements of consumption and real money holdings are depicted in Figure 5. The decrease in government spending brings about an excess supply in the goods market. This raises the real interest rate. Assuming a constant rate of inflation, the increase in the real interest rate causes the substitution from real money holdings to consumption (A → B in Figure 5). However, the increase in the utility level makes the movement of real money holdings rather ambiguous (A → C in Figure 5).

3. 4. Capital flows and international indebtedness

In this section, we will study the determination of international indebtedness positions in the stationary state.

---

5) *Mundell* 1963, p. 283.

6) See Appendix 2.

By substituting the government budget constraint (9) into (7), and setting $\dot{a} = 0$, we can obtain the domestic country's budget constraint in the stationary state,

(31) $y + \bar{r}\,\bar{b} - \bar{c} = 0.$

Also, we obtain for the foreign country,

(32) $y^* + \bar{r}\,\bar{b}^* - \bar{c}^* = 0.$

In light of the commodity market clearing condition, we can see,

(33) $\bar{b} + \bar{b}^* = 0.$

This is the equilibrium condition of the world bond market.

In addition, we know that consumption is determined by both the real and nominal interest rate in the stationary state. Set,

(34) $\bar{c} = C(\bar{r}, \bar{\pi})$

(35) $\bar{c}^* = C^*(\bar{r}, \bar{\pi}^*).$

If we hold money growth rates μ, μ^* constant, we can show the international indebtedness position in Figure 6. In this case, we assume the domestic country is the creditor.

Now, let us study the impact of monetary and real shocks on international indebtedness. First, let us consider a monetary shock.

Assume that the money growth rate of the domestic country is increased. Differentiating (31), we obtain,

(36) $d\bar{b}/d\mu = (d\bar{c}/d\mu - \bar{b} \;.\; d\bar{r}/d\mu)/\bar{r}.$

As we know, $d\bar{c}/d\mu > 0$, $d\bar{r}/d\mu < 0$, and if we suppose, $\bar{b} \gtreqless 0$ at the initial position, we can conclude $d\bar{b}/d\mu > 0$.

Next, let us consider the real shock. Similarly, we obtain,

(37) $d\bar{b}/dy = (d\bar{c}/dy - \bar{b} \cdot d\bar{r}/dy - 1)/\bar{r}$.

Also, we can attain a definite result, if $\bar{b} \geqq 0$.

Since $dc/dy < 1$ and $d\bar{r}/dy > 0$, we can conclude $d\bar{b}/dy < 0$.

4. Concluding remarks

In this paper, we have analyzed the effects of real and monetary shocks regarding the real interest rate, consumption, money holdings and international indebtedness under the stationary state condition. We were able to obtain the following main results.

First, an increase in the money growth rate reduces the world rate of real interest and utility levels of both countries. This result challenges the conventional view that monetary shocks are insulated by the change in the exchange rate. In fact, even monetary shocks are transmitted to another country through the channel of the world rate of real interest.

Second, a reduction in domestic government expenditure increases the world rate of real interest and utility levels of both countries. In this model, a reduction in government expenditures is equivalent to an increase in output. A rise in real interest is necessary to equate demand to supply in the goods market, because consumption is an increasing function of the real interest rate. This property of the consumption function stems from the key assumption on the time preference function. Without this *Uzawa*-type (increasing) time preference function of utility, we cannot conduct the analysis of the stationary state properly.

Appendix

a) Monetary shock

Setting $d\mu > 0$, $d\mu^* = dy = dy^* = 0$, we can solve (30). The determinant of the coefficient matrix,

$$\Delta = \delta^{*\prime}(\delta' U_m - x_m)(x_c{}^* U_m{}^* - x_m{}^* U_c{}^*) + \delta'(\delta^{*\prime} U_m{}^* - x_m{}^*)(x_c U_m - x_m U_c)$$

is positive.

$$d\bar{r}/d\mu = \delta'\delta^{*\prime} U_m (x_m{}^* U_c{}^* - x_c{}^* U_m{}^*)/\Delta < 0$$

$$d\bar{c}/d\mu = \delta' U_m (\delta^{*\prime} U_m{}^* - x_m{}^*)/\Delta > 0$$

$$d\bar{c}^*/d\mu = \delta' U_m (x_m{}^* - \delta^{*\prime} U_m{}^*)/\Delta < 0$$

$$d\bar{m}/d\mu = [\delta^{*\prime}(U_c{}^* x_m{}^* - U_m{}^* x_c{}^*) + \delta' U_c (x_m{}^* - \delta^{*\prime} U_m{}^*)]/\Delta < 0$$

$$d\bar{m}^*/d\mu = \delta' U_m (\delta^{*\prime} U_c{}^* - x_c{}^*)/\Delta \gtreqless 0$$

$$|d\bar{r}/d\mu| = \delta' U_m A/[(\delta' U_m - x_m)A + B] < 1$$

where $A = \delta^{*\prime}(U_m{}^* x_c{}^* - U_c{}^* x_m{}^*) > 0$

$B = \delta'(\delta^{*\prime} U_m{}^* - x_m{}^*)(U_m x_c - U_c x_m) > 0$

b) Real shock

Set $dy > 0$, $d\mu = d\mu^* = dy^* = 0$, and solve (30). We get the following results:

$$d\bar{r}/dy = [\delta'\delta^{*\prime}(U_m x_c - U_c x_m)(U_m^* x_c^* - U_c^* x_m^*)]/\Delta > 0$$

$$d\bar{c}/dy = \delta^{*\prime}(\delta' U_m - x_m)(U_m^* x_c^* - U_c^* x_m^*)/\Delta > 0$$

$$d\bar{c}^*/dy = \delta'(\delta^{*\prime} U_m - x_m^*)(U_m x_c - U_c x_m)/\Delta > 0$$

$$d\bar{m}/dy = \delta^{*\prime}(\delta' U_c - x_c)(U_m^* x_c^* - U_c^* x_m^*)/\Delta \gtreqless 0$$

$$d\bar{m}^*/dy = \delta'(\delta^{*\prime} U_c - x_c^*)(U_m x_c - U_c x_m)/\Delta \gtreqless 0$$

and

$$d\bar{c}/dy = [(\delta' U_m - x_m)A]/[(\delta' U_m - x_m)A + B] < 1$$

where A and B are the same as above.

Literature

Frankel, J. A./*Razin*, A., Government Spending, Debt, and International Economic Interdependence, Economic Journal 95, 1985

Frankel, J. A./*Razin*, A., Fiscal Policies in the World Economy, Journal of Political Economy 94, 1986

Hamada, K., The Political Economy of International Monetary Interdependence, Cambridge, Mass. (MIT Press) 1985

Mundell, R. A., Inflation and Real Interest, Journal of Political Economy 74, 1963

Obstfeld, M., Macroeconomic Policy, Exchange-Rate Dynamics, and Optimal Asset Accumulation, Journal of Policital Economy 89, 1981

Rodriguez, A., Long-Run Effects of Monetary Policy within a Two-Country Model, Journal of International Economics 12, 1982

Uzawa, H., Time Preference, the Consumption Function, and Optimal Asset Holdings Value, Capital and Growth: Papers in Honour of Sir John *Hicks*, in: J. N. *Wolfe* (ed.), Chicago (Aldine Publishing Company) 1968

Figure 1

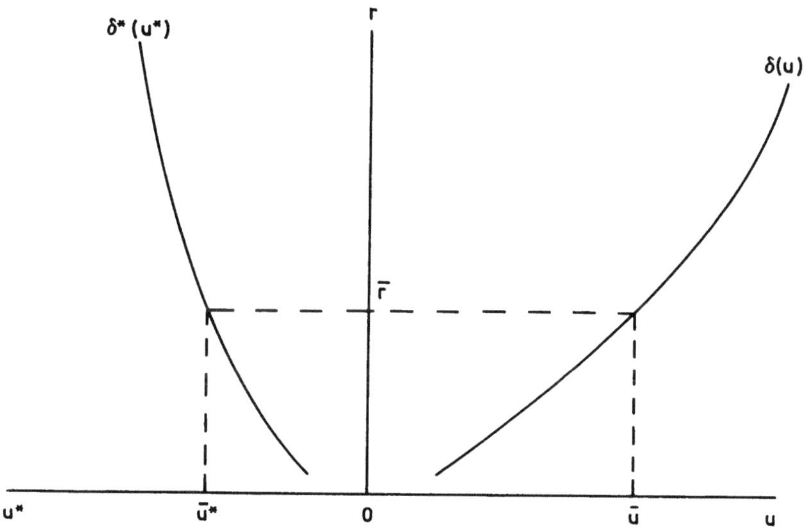

Figure 2

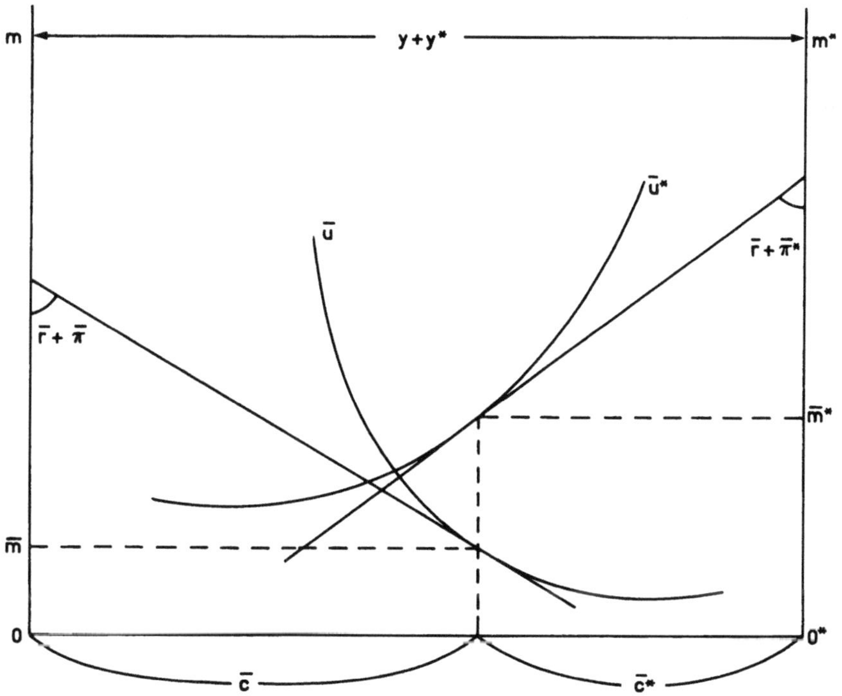

Figure 3

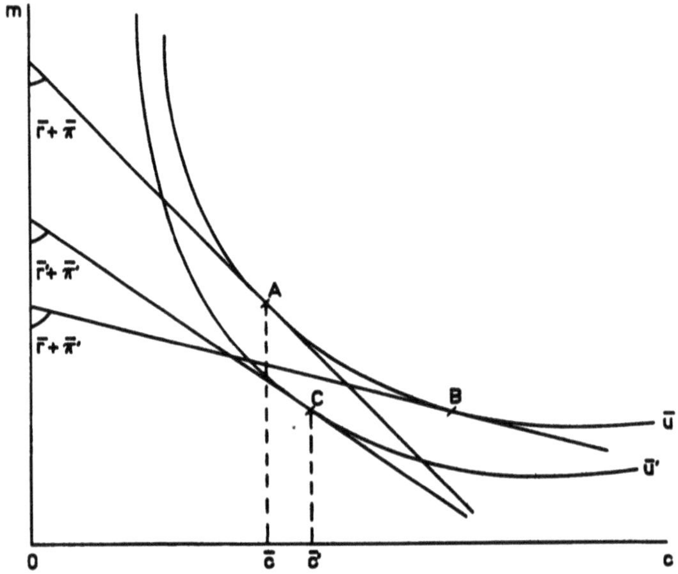

Figure 4

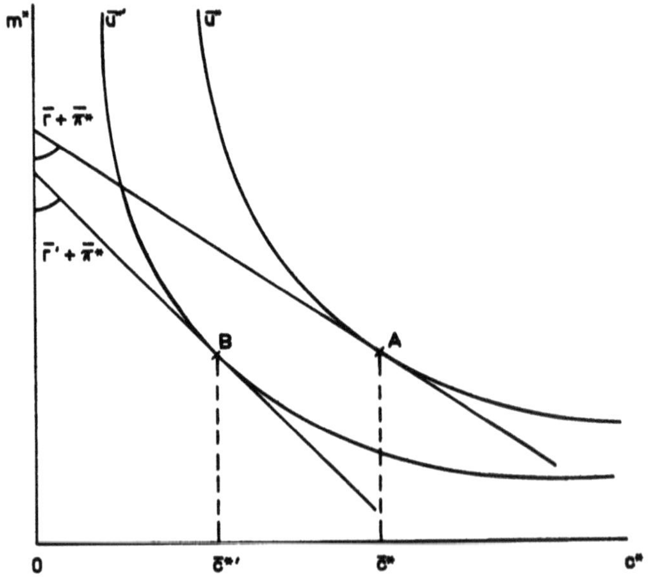

Figure 5

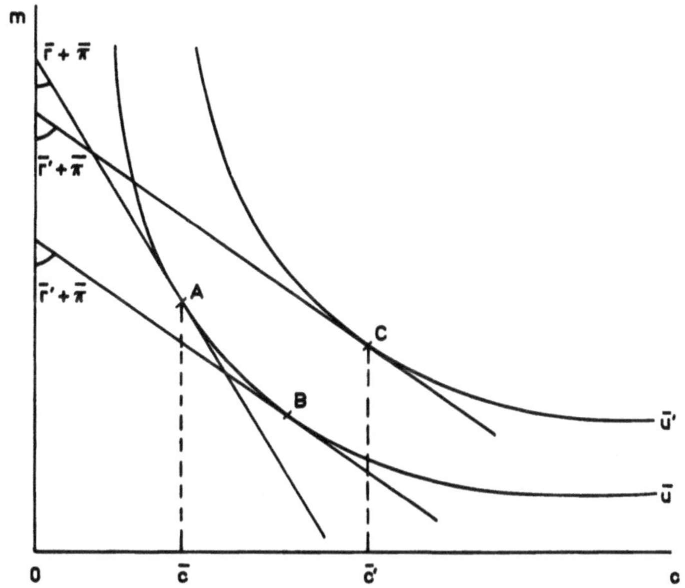

Figure 6

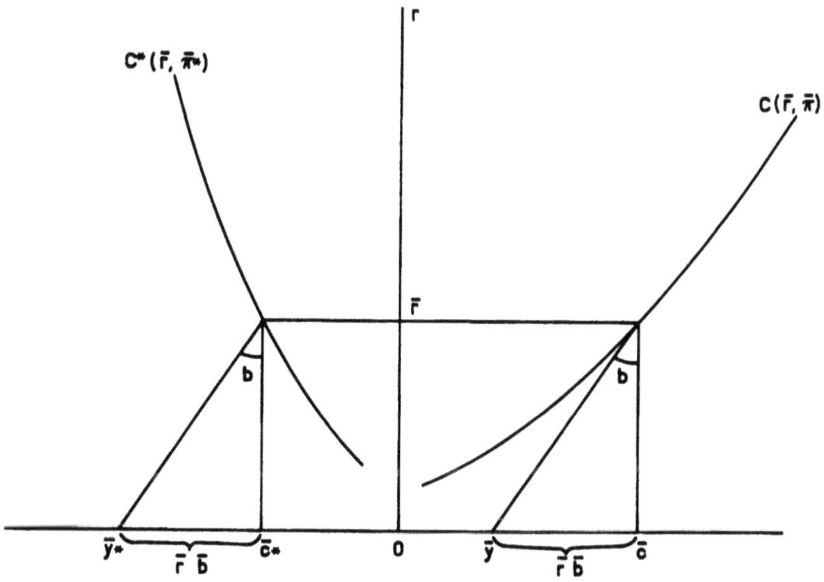

International Capital Movements and Distribution of Income

Alois Oberhauser

1. Problem

The current accounts of single countries are usually unbalanced. They show large surplusses and deficits. (Net) capital exports or (net) capital imports respectively, correspond to these, if interventions of the central banks on the money markets are ignored or are simply regarded as a special form of international capital movement. During the last years, countries with especially high surplusses in the current accounts - relative to the national product - and therefore equally high net capital exports, included Japan and the Federal Republic of Germany, but also threshhold countries like South Korea or Taiwan. In 1987, the surplusses in the current accounts amounted to 3.5 % of the gross national product for Japan and 4.0 % for the Federal Republic of Germany. In the early eighties both countries still were net capital importers. Between 1980 and 1987 the quota of the balance of current accounts in relation to the national product therefore rose by 4.5 percentage points in Japan and by 6.0 percentage points in the FRG.

Looking at the world as a whole, surplusses in the current accounts and corresponding capital exports of the "surplus"-countries equal deficits and corresponding capital imports of the "deficit"-countries. Among the "deficit"-countries there are not only developing countries, but also, since 1982, the United States of America. The U.S. current account surplus of +0.1 % of the national product in 1980 (1.9 billion $) fell to a deficit of 3.6 % in 1986 (160 billion $). Such high and constantly changing imbalances of the current accounts[1] are coupled with multiple economic effects and problems, such as the international debt crisis and the drop of the dollar exchange rate. The following considerations will only deal with a

---

[1] Deutsches Institut für Wirtschaftsforschung 1988, p. 2. International Financial Statistics. World Economic Outlook, October 1987.

small fraction of the entire spectrum. An aspect which is normally disregarded, namely the distributional effects which accompany international capital movements[2], will be examined. These distributional effects are of considerable quantitative importance and should therefore not be disregarded, neither in distribution theory nor in distribution policy. However, the policy of international economics has, till now, seldomly been regarded as distribution policy or even being relevant to distribution.

To limit the extensive subject matter, this study will only deal with a country with net capital exports and corresponding surplusses in the current accounts. Specifically, increases of capital exports will be examined. The opposite situation, namely capital imports (or decreasing capital exports), will not be dealt with explicitly. The distributional effects of capital imports are normally just opposites of the ones being deduced.

2. Factors determining international capital movement

In economies with free international capital movements a great number of factors determine the international flow of capital. They normally do not all work in the same direction, but quite often exactly opposite to each other. This is pointed out by the movements in the balance of payments of the FRG in 1986. The effects of the surplusses of 81 billion DM in the current accounts were amplified by long-term capital imports of 36 billion DM. These were counterbalanced by short-term capital exports of 105 billion DM (and a few smaller compensating items).

The following deliberations will not deal with the different factors that determine international capital movement[3]. It will suffice to differentiate between two large groups:

- Capital flows which depend on the movements in the current accounts. Exports and imports are often only undertaken in connection with international credit grants.
- Many international capital flows are quite independent from direct transactions in the balance of current accounts. This is especially

---

[2] See also *Scholl* 1986.

[3] For this see *Niehaus* 1984, pp. 195 - 214.

true for those capital assets in foreign countries, which resulted out of differing interest rates, diverging profit margins or exchange rate expectations.

Assuming that exchange rates are determined by free markets, both types of international capital movement influence their formation. Therefore, the exchange rates not only depend on the prices of the exported and imported goods and services, but also on the factors which determine the international flow of capital.

3. Types of distributional effects

The international flow of capital is coupled with quite a few different distributional effects. Relevant are, first, the effects on the level of the national product[4]. If it is assumed that there will not be permanent full employment, then each real level of the national product will also be determined by the balance of the current accounts, the rates of exchange and the level of interest, which is influenced by the international capital flows. Since the (net) national product is equivalent to the sum of incomes, these relations are also important for the distribution of income. Economic growth of a country is also influenced by these relations. This is even true - as will be shown later - if the export of capital is not detrimental to domestic investments.

The national-product-effects have been widely discussed in literature[5]. The following considerations will therefore not concentrate on the effects on macroeconomic income, but instead deal with the effects on the distribution of this income. It is assumed that the income level is otherwise determined, whereby net capital exports and their corresponding surplusses in the current accounts also have an influence.

The analysis of the distributional effects will focus on the distribution of income between the two big social groups, namely wage earners and profit earners. Consequently, the development of

---

[4] In the following, except for the last part, there will be no differentiation between the national product and the domestic product.

[5] Among others: *Machlup* 1965, esp. p. 130; *Laursen/Metzler* 1950, p. 281; *Stern* 1973, esp. pp. 166 and 242; *Scammell* 1974, esp. p. 370.

the wage and profit quota is of importance for this study. The distributional effects within the two aggregates will not be taken into account, even if they are of substantial importance for the individuals involved. In view of the aggregational distribution, we must distinguish between three different aspects:

- First, it has to be taken into account that if the national product is given, surplusses in the current accounts will reduce the amount of goods available domestically. This influences the distribution of income substantially. The amount of net capital exports consists entirely of drawings from private savings.

- Secondly, these effects are overlapped and supplemented by changes of the terms of trade, which include exchange rate fluctuations. Since international capital flows also influence exchange rates, these distributional effects will be considered separately. Changes in the terms of trade are coupled with quantitative effects on the amount of goods available domestically. These quantitative effects are not reflected in the nominal balance of current accounts. They may either be regarded separately, or one has to consider real terms in the current accounts. Despite the difficulty of separating these in reality, we shall in the following distinguish mentally between the two possibilities for reasons of clarity.

- Lastly, there is quite a different sort of distributional effects - namely those which are coupled with the foreign wealth of an economy. This wealth is equal to gross foreign wealth minus foreign commitments. International capital movements change the amount of foreign wealth. This wealth normally leads to returns, which are influenced by different factors, such as the level of foreign interest or the rates of exchange. Movements in exchange rates also influence the value of foreign wealth - measured in domestic currency. Such value changes may quantitatively far exceed the yearly returns. Empirically, this can be seen as a result of the large fluctuations of the exchange rates during the last years.

We use the *Kaldor*ian macroeconomic model of income distribution as an analytical instrument to analyse these three distributional effects. We also include foreign economic interrelations, which are mostly neglected when dealing with this model.

The study proceeds in three steps, according to the three distributional effects that have to be analyzed. First, we will ask, how increasing capital exports affect the distribution of income between the big social groups if terms of trade are given. Secondly, we include changes of the terms of trade. In a third step we add the distributional effects of returns from foreign wealth and of changes in the value of this wealth induced by exchange rate movements.

4. Distributional effects of net capital exports with given terms of trade

If we disregard currency transactions of the central banks, then net capital exports will, as has been mentioned, always correspond to surplusses in the current accounts. The capital exports may be the reason for the surplusses, if they induce the foreign countries to buy more domestic goods. On the other hand, these capital exports may result in surplusses in the current accounts. This may happen if the additional foreign demand for goods and services is coupled with the granting of loans to foreign countries.

Quite independent from what causes the surplusses of the current accounts, they always - in relation to the national product - reduce the amount of goods available domestically. However, it is possible that the level of the national product is influenced by the surplusses in the current accounts. They may contribute to a rise of the national product in an economy where there is not full employment. In that case the domestic use of goods will not necessarily have to be reduced. Indeed, it may be possible that multiplier and accelerator effects bring about an increase of the national product which is several times the amount of the increase of the surplusses of the current accounts. These interrelations will, however, not be further discussed[6].

The effects on the distribution of income are independent from the effects on the national income. In particular, distributional effects result from the fact that as to the amount of current account surplusses, income does not constitute demand domestically and therefore has to be saved. Consequently, foreign wealth builds up.

---

[6] To be compared with my contribution to one of the previous Nagoya-Freiburg-Seminars: *Oberhauser* 1980, pp. 303-319.

Net capital exports therefore always take up parts of the domestic savings volume and -assuming constant governmen lending[7] - of the private savings volume. In macroeconomic terms the following identity is always true: Private saving (S_{pr}) or private accumulation of wealth (WA_{pr}) is identical to the sum of private net investments (I_{pr}^{n}), public deficit (D_G) and the balance of current accounts (X -M):

$$(1)\quad S_{pr} \equiv WA_{pr} \equiv I_{pr}^{n} + D_G + (X-M)$$

It is therefore decisive, whether an increase of capital exports will, by inducing increases in the level of interest, lead to crowding-out of private investments. In literature this assumption is often made, but it has been contradicted to a large extent by empirical experience[8]. In the FRG, for instance, the increase of the surplus of the current accounts by 6 percentage points of the national product between 1980 and 1986 was accompanied by an increase of the profit share of national income of almost 5 percentage points, with a corresponding reduction of the wage share[9]. The investment quota was reduced a little during this time. Yet, this reduction was not motivated by interest changes, since interest was lowered during this time. Due to a policy aimed at stopping the increase of the public deficit, the deficit quota was also reduced. Nevertheless, it may be concluded that in the FRG the macroeconomically necessary additional savings for the additional capital exports were predominantly supplied by the redistribution of income in favor of entrepreneurs. Similarities may be observed in Japan.

---

7) This will always be assumed in the following.

8) Additionally I may point out the following aspect: If complete crowding-out would take place, then surplusses in the current accounts would not have an expanding influence on an underemployed economy. This also contradicts empirical evidence.

9) The newest calculations of the Council of Economic Advisors show that the wage quota fell from 73.5 % in 1980 to 68.8 % in 1986. At the same time the income from wealth of private households rose by 1.2 % and the income from profits in stricter sense (after subtraction of hypothetically calculated entrepreneurial wages) by 4.6 %. See Sachverständigenrat 1987/88, p. 110.

These empirical events may be explained with the help of following theoretical considerations. As the *Kaldor*ian macroeconomic theory of distribution has shown, the level of entrepreneurial income and returns from wealth (in short: profits), under the assumption of a given national product, depends on the structural use of the income and on the saving patterns of wage earners and entrepreneurs. The *Keynes*ian equation of distribution exemplifies these connections. According to this equation, the net income from entrepeneurship and wealth (P_n) is mainly determined by the three elements which constitute private accumulation of wealth and which form the right hand part of Equation (1). We have to add entrepreneurial consumption (C_P) and subtract the savings of wage earners (S_W).

$$(2)\quad P_n = I^n_{pr} + D_G + (X-M) + C_P - S_W$$

By making behavioral assumptions, the macroeconomic theory of distribution tries to clear up how changes of single factors will affect other factors. In this case, we have to ask, what effects additional capital exports (or additional surplusses of the current accounts) will have on other factors. Surplusses of the current accounts are not only part of private savings, their importance results much more from the fact that they absorb a part of the produced volume of goods. In this context, we cannot discuss all the relevant interrelations; only the explanatory approaches will be shown.

If we assume an adequate elasticity of money supply, which in reality and particularly in underemployed economies is usually the case, then additional surplusses of the current accounts will lead to redistributional effects in favor of entrepreneurial income. This way, savings adapt to the rising demand for investable funds. In a fully employed economy additional foreign demand will induce increases in the price level, which expands profits. These profits are (at least in the short-term) not distributed. They form part of private savings. In an underemployed economy the necessary additional savings partly result from the rise in income induced by the additional demand, but also partly from a redistribution of income in favor of profits. Under certain circumstances, these redistributions may be possible without increases in the price level, as fixed costs per produced item go down with increased utilisation of capacity and, thus, the profit margin per item rises.

Except in the case of a very restrictive monetary policy, it is quite improbable that domestic investments are reduced by rising foreign demand. Instead, the propensity to invest rises with foreign demand. Even a certain increase of the interest level is thereby more or less compensated. Furthermore, the increase of profits will stimulate investments.

Net capital exports and surplusses in the current accounts therefore change the relations of distribution - favorably for profit and unfavorably for wage earners. The additional private accumulation of wealth (in foreign countries) largely goes to the profiteers.

The most important conclusion of the macroeconomic distribution theory is the fact that private savings - for which private investments, public deficit and the balance of current accounts then would have to compete via changes of interest rates - are not determined by the amount private households decide to save. Private saving is a much more dependent variable, which adapts through changes in distribution. It is therefore not as Hisao *Kanamori* and *Kamppeter* believe[10], that a surplus of savings in Japan, which once financed the public deficit, will now, after these deficits have been reduced, flow to foreign countries as capital exports, and thereby finance the budget deficits in the USA. The profit quota would have decreased if there had not been surplusses in the current accounts. Macroeconomically an oversupply of savings is not possible (ex post).

On the other hand, it would be wrong to view the changes of the distributional relations as the only adaptive mechanism of savings. The classical interest mechanism and the *Keynes*ian income mechanism also play their part. How these three mechanisms are interrelated and by which factors they are coordinated, is still quite unclear[11].

10) *Kamppeter* 1988, p. 16.

11) *Oberhauser* 1988, p. 97.

5. Distributional effects of changing terms of trade

The distributional effects of the current accounts are overlapped by changes of the terms of trade, which include all real changes of exchange rates and of international exchange relations.

The terms of trade are influenced and determined by a multitude of different factors. For the distribution of income it is particularly important that changes in the terms of trade prove to be changes in the amounts of imported and exported goods and services, which means that not only changes of current accounts, but also the amount of goods available domestically, are influenced. Even with a close to constant balance of current accounts, serious changes in the terms of trade may occur.

The quantitative importance of these terms-of-trade effects may best be illustrated by examples. The price increase of oil during the two oil crisis and the increase in the prices of raw materials forced import dependent countries like Japan and the FRG to deliver more export goods for the same quantity of raw materials - their terms of trade worsened. Normally such developments also influence the current accounts, but there are no fixed interrelations between the changes of the terms of trade and the changes in the current accounts. Both effects overlap. Whether they add up or compensate each other, depends on a row of other determining factors. These interrelations will not be examined here. Important for distributional effects is that both facts influence the amount of goods available domestically.

Similarly strong effects may occur if the terms of trade improve. The fall of the exchange rate of the dollar and the decrease in prices of raw materials led to a decrease of the price level in the FRG in 1986 and 1987, although wage costs per item rose. The pure terms-of-trade effect, according to the calculations of the German Economic Advisory Council, amounted to nearly 3 % of the national product in 1986 and 0.9 % in 1987[12]. In relation to the domestically available national product the terms-of-trade effects were partly

12) Sachverständigenrat 1987/88, p. 111.

compensated by increases of the surplus of the current accounts. Similar effects may be observed in Japan or Switzerland[13].

Distribution depends on these terms-of-trade effects in much the same way as on the above discussed current account effects. We again abstain from possible changes of the domestically produced national product. An improvement of the terms of trade - assuming other variables as constant - implies that there will be more goods available domestically, a deterioration means less available goods.

Changes of the terms of trade are not reflected in the nominal amounts of the national product or in the *Keynes*ian equation of distribution, which is based on the nominal national product. They therefore have to be considered additionally.

In the macroeconomic theory of distribution this is done the following way. The normal deductions of this theory describe the distribution of the nominal national product. Changes in the price structure and the thereby following quantitative effects are not regarded. If the terms of trade change, however, then the price structure does change. We may include these terms of trade effects in the *Kaldor*-model by calculating the real values (i. e. net of price changes) of every single component. The real influence of the terms of trade on the distributional latitude is thereby registered. In this way, the real balance of (X-M) not only shows the level of the nominal balance of current accounts, but also the change of the internal distributional latitude, which results from changes in the terms of trade. These terms of trade effects become even clearer if they, like in this paper, are considered separately.

As empirical evidence shows, such changes in the terms of trade have a serious influence on the distributional latitude of an economy. They may be so great that the increases of yearly productivity may either be more than absorbed by their deterioration, or be more than doubled by their improvement[14].

---

13) *Landmann* 1984, p. 179

14) This is the only aspect of the macroeconomic theory of distribution which the German Economic Advisory Council includes in its concept of cost neutral wage policy. It disregards, however, the importance of the surplusses of the current accounts and of the other relevant macroeconomic factors. See also *Güssregen* 1974.

International capital movements have a considerable influence on the degree of changes of the terms of trade. Net capital exports are not only to be viewed in the current accounts, they also have strong effects on the rates of exchange. We assume that these interrelations are known. Each net capital import tends to devaluate the domestic currency, each net capital export has the opposite effect.

The huge distributional effects which are linked to the two factors already mentioned may be demonstrated with the example of the USA. The policy of high interest rates and the expectations of a rising dollar led not only to strong capital imports into the USA, but also, until 1985, to an increase of the exchange rate of the dollar against the DM and the yen by more than 100 % measured against the low watermark of the rates in 1980. To the extent of the deficits in the current accounts and of the improvement of the terms of trade the USA in those years were able to increase domestic consumption and domestic investments above the amount of goods produced at home. It may be left open, whether or not during this time the high and favorable imports were paid for with a lesser expansion of employment.

The burden on the American economy grew much bigger after the peak of the exchange rate of the dollar had passed. The deficit in the current accounts has still not decreased. The value of the dollar, however, sank rapidly - to less than half measured against the yen or the DM. In real terms much more had to be exported for the same amount of imports. The amount of goods available at home diminished correspondingly.

This, viewed separately, had positive effects on employment. These were, however, at least partly compensated by the, in international comparison, high domestic interest rate level, which was necessary to make the capital imports possible. The high interest rates were also caused by the inflationary tendencies of a deteriorating exchange rate.

In such a situation the pressure on the exchange rate increases, because foreign capital owners are induced to withdraw capital. The frantic and little successful endeavours of the central banks to stabilize the exchange rate of the dollar shifted parts of foreign U.S.

debt from private to government lenders[15]. These events are also relevant for distribution.

During the last few years, Japan and the FRG have experienced effects which were quite the opposite of those in the USA. It may suffice in this context to mention that the changes of the distributionary latitude caused by the changes of the terms of trade were enormous.

These correlations also have ramifications on the distributional relations between wage earners and entrepreneurs. Surplusses in the current accounts need corresponding domestic savings, while changes of the terms of trade are not, at least not directly, coupled with the building up of wealth. Except for ramifications on the national product and the current accounts, they change, rather, the amount of goods available domestically. An improvement of the terms of trade implies a corresponding increase of this amount. It is not probable that the entrepreneurs will then invest more, which would change the distributional relations. Only if the prices of raw materials are falling, it is not wholly impossible that private investment is stimulated. With the rising domestic exchange rate, however, the international sales prospects of companies go down. Their propensity to invest will therefore rather be reduced.

The increase of the amount of domestically used goods will therefore normally increase the possibilities of consumption, which means above all an increase of real income of wage earners. Real wages can increase more than the increase in productivity, which, for instance, was the case in the FRG during 1986 and 1987.

Deteriorations of the terms of trade on the other hand decrease the distributionary latitude especially unfavorable for wage earners. Examples are given for this in the FRG as well. During the oil crisis in the beginning of the 1980's, real wages were reduced in spite of high increases of nominal wages. In those years the national product stagnated because of a cyclical downswing, while a larger part of it had to be used in exchange for imports.

---

15) In 1987, for instance, the German central bank (Deutsche Bundesbank) financed approxemately one half of the balance of the current accounts, that in the previous year changed only slightly, by buying foreign currencies.

On the whole, one may conclude that distributional effects which result from changes of the terms of trade, are no less important than those which result from changes in the current accounts. International capital movement influences both factors. Quantitatively they are ramifications on the distributional latitude, which in single years may well exceed those of increased productivity. Improvement of the terms of trade always - viewed separately - increases the distributional latitude in favor of the wage earners; deterioration of the terms of trade decreases it. These distributional effects may work in the same direction as changes in the current account. It seems therefore quite necessary to consider and compare both effects in the scope of distributional policy.

6. Returns from foreign wealth and domestic distribution of income

Another kind of distributional effects shall be pointed out. The effects depend on the amount of foreign wealth which was accumulated by former capital exports (including changes of value). The wealth held in foreign countries must be weighed against foreign wealth domestically. In the following we will only regard net foreign wealth. International capital relations have boomed during the last years, and as a result typical debtor and creditor countries have developed.

Foreign wealth normally yields returns, in form of interest, dividends and profits. Only those returns which are transfered back to the domestic market are part of the service transactions in the current accounts. The following considerations will deal with those transfered returns. The net capital returns are not of very high quantitative importance in the FRG (6.4 billion DM in 1987). They do, however, play an important role in countries with relatively high net foreign wealth, as, for instance, Japan (the equivalent of 26 billion DM in 1987) or formerly Great Britain[16].

The transfered (but also the non-transfered) returns of foreign wealth constitute claims on the foreign national product. Those claims which rely on transfered returns, will only be put into effect through goods, if the receiving country accepts deficits in the balance

---

16) See also Deutsche Bundesbank 1988, p. 23.

of trade in corresponding amounts. In this case the domestically available amount of goods will exceed the domestic product[17].

If such transactions of goods take place, then the distributional effects will depend on the recipients' utilization of those returns from foreign wealth for own consumption or investments. If we assume that the recipients are in general companies or earners of high incomes, then we may assume a relatively small marginal propensity to consume with this sort of income. Moreover, returns will rarely be used for additional domestic investments. Under these circumstances, the corresponding goods are indirectly available for other consumers. One may assume from the macroeconomic distributional relations spoken of above that, with given domestic production, the real income of wage earners has to rise[18].

The profits of central banks from foreign capital assets constitute a special case, if there is a real transfer to the domestic economy. If these profits are transfered to the government, then it has these profits at its disposal for the equivalent in goods. We obtain distributional effects in favor of the government. These make it possible to spend more or tax less. In that way the taxpayers indirectly would be favored.

The previous assumption, that the returns of the foreign wealth would be compensated in goods by deficits in the balance of trade, is probably an exception. We have to expect, rather, that in Japan and the FRG those returns, except those of the central banks, will appear as additional currency offers on the currency markets. This will tend to increase the exchange rate of the domestic currency. This increase leads to distributional effects of the kind we discussed in part 5 of this paper.

Apart from the direct returns of foreign wealth, also the changes of value of this wealth - measured in domestic currency - are relevant for distribution. Foreign wealth, in contrast to domestic wealth, has additional changes of value, next to "normal" value changes, because of fluctuations of exchange rates. That means, an

---

17) The national product includes the transfered returns from foreign wealth.

18) For most countries in the world the opposite is true, as they are net capital debtors (have negative foreign wealth).

increase of the exchange rate of the domestic currency - assuming other variables are unchanged -increases the value of foreign wealth; a decrease of the exchange rate lowers it.

First, this only influences the asset value of the owners of foreign wealth. For the economy as a whole and for the distribution of income, such changes in value are only relevant because they also influence the international flow of capital. Expected revaluations of the foreign currency cause the owners of foreign wealth to avoid transfering this wealth and its returns back to the domestic market. Expected devaluations, however, lead to a withdrawal of capital assets from foreign countries. Both actions aggravate the exchange rate fluctuations and amplify the terms of trade effects we have spoken of.

7. Results and distributional conclusions

The results of our considerations may be summed up as follows:

- International capital movements have quantitatively very important ramifications on the distribution of income. Within a few years, these capital movements may be responsible for serious changes in the distributional relations. Thus, international capital movements have at least the same importance for the distribution of income as changes of private investment or of public deficit, which, because of the macroeconomic distributional relations, have similar distributional effects. The macroeconomic theory of distribution, however, almost always disregards international capital flows.

- Private investments, public deficit and international capital movements give rise to distributional effects by having an influence on the specific uses of the national product. These are distributional effects which result from the economic process which are rarely aimed at and controlled politically. They consist of repercussions on the level of the national product, which were not examined here, and of changing distribution quotas.

- International capital movement influences the distribution quotas in three ways: If we only look at net capital exports, then these are equivalent to the surplusses of the current accounts, as long as the central banks do not carry out currency transactions. During the periods in question there have to be additional savings to the amount of the surplusses of the current accounts. Generally, we may assume that private investments will not be reduced, savings will adapt to changes in the distribution of income. Income as a whole will be redistributed in favour of the entrepreneurs, which means an increase of the profit quota and a decrease of the wage quota.

- The changes of distribution of goods are modified by changes of the terms of trade. Net capital exports and surplusses of the current accounts may be coupled with either an improvement or a deterioration of the terms of trade. Therefore, the consequences of the changes of distribution which result from changes of the balance of current accounts are either amplified or diminished.

- Of quantitatively lesser importance is a third effect, which results from the transfered returns of the net foreign capital of an economy. As long as there is no direct utilisation of the amount of these returns of foreign goods and services, increases of the exchange rate and consequently of the terms of trade will occur.

If international capital movements have such strong influence on the distribution of income, then they should be considered by distribution policy. Until now this has only happened rudimentarily. In distribution policy, neither the collective wage bargainers, nor the government have tried to include foreign economical facts and international capital movements in their decisions. This, however, is only one aspect of the general shortcoming, that macroeconomic distributionary relations up till now only seldomly have served as a basis for the actions of distribution policy.

Distribution policy, which considers international capital movements, could use the following standards of orientation: It would have to try to work towards prevention of high surplusses of the current accounts. Only during periods of unemployment it could be necessary to allow such surplusses as a means of increasing employment. Even then the fear remains that the cutback of these surplusses, which different economic forces and foreign interests are working towards, will hardly be achieved without negative consequences for employment. Strong fluctuations of the current accounts are therefore problematic in view of both employment policy and distribution policy.

Similar adaptionary difficulties could arise from quick changes of the terms of trade, which are strongly influenced by the international movement of capital. Notwithstanding the (under circumstances) positive distributional effects of terms of trade improvements, strong fluctuations will have a negative influence because of the necessary structural adaptions. It would therefore be favorable, from the viewpoint of distribution policy, to stabilize the terms of trade. Economic policy could try to achieve this stabilization.

In reality, however, it probably has to be assumed that economies with freely convertable currencies will not be able to politically steer foreign economic events. All the more it is necessary to regard the distributional effects coupled with those economic events when calculating distributional latitude. Otherwise similar negative effects as with nominal wage policy will, in the end, occur for all concerned.

References

Deutsche Bundesbank, Kapitalertragszahlungen zwischen der Bundesrepublik Deutschland und dem Ausland, in: Monatsberichte Deutsche Bundesbank, April 1988

Deutsches Institut für Wirtschaftsforschung, Grundlinien der Wirtschaftsentwicklung 1988, Weekly Report No. 1/1988

Güssregen, N., Kostenniveauneutrale Lohnpolitik und ihre verteilungspolitischen Implikationen, Frankfurt/M., Bern 1974

Kamppeter, W., Endaka - die japanische Wirtschaft nach der Aufwertungskrise. Forschungsinstitut der Friedrich-Ebert-Stiftung 1988

Landmann, O., Löhne, Preise, Einkommen und Beschäftigung in der offenen Volkswirtschaft, in: Der Keynesianismus, Volume V, Berlin 1984

Laursen, S./*Metzler*, L. A., Flexible Exchange Rates and the Theory of Employment, in: The Review of Economics and Statistics, Volume 32, No. 4, November 1950

Machlup, F., International Trade and the National Income Multiplier, New York 1965

Niehaus, J., International Monetary Economics, Oxford 1984

Oberhauser, A., Entwicklungshilfe als Mittel der Stabilitätspolitik in Rezessionsperioden, in: Th. *Dams*/K. *Jojima* (eds.), Ausgewählte Probleme internationaler Wirtschaftsbeziehungen, Berlin 1980

Oberhauser, A., Änderungen in der Einkommensverteilung und Zinsbildung. Eine notwendige Ergänzung der Zinstheorie, in: Herausforderungen der Wirtschaftspolitik, Berlin 1988

Sachverständigenrat, Jahresgutachten 1987/88

Scammell, W. M., International Trade and Payments, London 1974

Scholl, R. C., Internationale Kapitalbewegungen, Leistungsbilanzsalden und inländische Ersparnisbildung bei flexiblen Wechselkursen, Frankfurt 1986

Stern, R. M., The Balance of Payments, London 1973

International Competition among Tax Systems? The Significance of Corporate Taxation for International Investment Decisions

Bernd Rohwer

1. Preface

For several years now, reforms in both income and corporate taxation have been enjoying a "boom". In Great Britain, France, Germany, Japan, Sweden and the U.S., reductions in income tax, and in some cases even in corporate taxation, have come into force. In Italy and Austria such steps are planned. The objective of these tax relief measures is not only to offer the domestic economic units additional incentives for performance and investments. In view of the increasing interdependency of national economies, the individual states also feel an increasing necessity to improve the attractiveness of their own countries as locations for international investment through more favorable fiscal arrangements. For this reason, many now speak of an international *"competition among the tax systems"*.

In this paper, the author will analyse to what degree taxation is actually significant for the choice of location for international direct investments. In an initial step, some quantitative results on the international differences in corporate taxation will be presented. The second step will be to examine to which extent these differences in the tax burden, together with other factors, influence the regional distribution of direct investments. This paper is limited to the flow of direct investments among industrial countries; the direct investments in developing and in threshhold countries, will not be considered here.

2. Comparison of corporate taxation in selected industrial countries

2.1. Basic problems

In international comparisons of corporate tax burdens, there are a number of delimitation and gauging problems of which many, to this day, have not been adequately solved. Empirical comparisons of effective tax burdens are therefore at best rough approximations.

a) First of all, one must decide *which corporate taxes are to be included* in a comparison. For investment decisions, the burden of direct taxes (i.e. taxes on profits, earnings and assets) is of greater relevance than the burden of indirect taxes since, in the case of the latter, one may assume that these will be largely passed on. Moreover, one must distinguish exactly according to the *different corporate forms* (capital stock companies or unincorporated firms) and *use of profits* (distribution, retention).

b) In the case of direct corporate taxes, the *formal incidence*, at best, can be determined. Statements on the effective incidence, namely the distribution of the tax burden after forward and backward shifting of taxes, are possible only to a limited extent at the national level; internationally there are also the problems of comparable micro- and macro-data. For clarity in this context, we will refer to a comparison of overall profit tax burden rates.

c) Even the comparison of the formal incidence creates difficulties: Unlike the tax rates, there are no sufficiently reliable data on comparably delimited *tax bases* for taxes on profit and on assets. Since the effects of tax concessions and possibilities for modification in the tax balance sheet (scope in the assessment of assets and stocks, reserves and provisions or losses carried over) on the tax base can only be ascertained very incompletely, the effective tax burden can at most be determined as a very rough estimate. Here too, for the present, one must be satisfied with simplifying model calculations or macroeconomic auxiliary indicators.

2.2. Empirical findings for selected industrial nations

The comparison of the *tax rate burden* is relatively unproblematical. Among the six countries under consideration here,

West Germany, France, Great Britain, Japan, the Netherlands and the U.S. (there are comparatively diversified data available for them[1]), the U.S. emerges relatively favorably in the taxation of *unincorporated companies*, while the Netherlands and (even after the most recent reform) Japan have particularly high marginal income tax rates (cf. Table 1). However, for our study, the taxation of *capital stock companies* is more decisive since by far the greatest share of international direct investments is made by them. Here we must distinguish between distributed and retained profits.

In the case of *distributed profits*, West Germany is in a relatively favorable position thanks to its full credit procedure, while double taxation of dividends, especially in the U.S., Japan and the Netherlands, leads to a heavier burden in these countries. However, one must remember that the profits paid abroad, which are initially subject to high taxation (36 % corporate income tax, 15 % capital gains tax and 10-15 % other earnings tax), can, as a rule, be credited only up to the rates of income tax applicable abroad; in the case of profit distributions to countries with low income tax rates (e.g., the U.S.), a loss of tax credit is incurred which, in this case, is greater than would be the case with profit distributions of, for example, British companies.

When comparing the burden of corporate income tax on *retained profits*, the order of the countries (cf. Table 1) is altered: here Great Britain is especially favorable while Japan and West Germany appear unfavorable. When including the other taxes on earnings and assets, the difference is even greater; in West Germany the trade and business assets taxes, and in Japan the corporate and gross assets taxes result in considerable additional burdens.

In some cases, model calculations that attempt to ascertain the *effective taxation* of corporate profits arrive at markedly different results. Let us first look at the international differences in the way some of the important components of the tax base are arranged.

In the case of the *depreciation arrangements*, the differences in both the fiscal write-off period as well as in the rates of depreciation

---

[1] Cf. especially *Fuest/Kroker* 1987a, 1987 b, 1987 c.

Table 1:

International Comparison of Corporate Taxation

Indicator	Year	USA	Japan	Germany	France	UK	Netherl.
tariff tax rate burden							
...of unincorporated companies with income tax (top rate)[1)4)]	1987	38,0	65,0	53,0	50,0	60,0 (40,0)	72,0
...of corporated companies							
with (corporate) income tax	1987						
a) retained profits[2)4)]		40,6	50,7	50,0	42,0	35,0	42,0
b) distributed profits[3)4)]		64,8	66,0	50,0	58,8	54,2	71,0
with (corporate) income tax, earnings and assets taxes (retained profits)[2)4)]	1987	46,0	63,7	66,2	62,9	35,0	42,0
effective tax burden							
...of corporated companies							
with income amd earnings taxes incl. depreciation conditions and investment subsidies[5)]	1983 (1986)	19,0	36,0	43 (39)	-	20 (25)	16,0
with direct taxes according to national accounts[6)]	1985	18,3	28,3	(19,3)	24,1	36,0	9,3
for comparison: estimates by Kay/Sen und Ifo[7)]	1980	27,0	27,0	22,0	25,0	38,0	-
...of real investment (marginal tax burden)[8)]	1986	31,0	20-30	39,8	-	37,4	-
additionally: taxes on corporate profits in % of GNP (OECD)	1984	2,07	5,78	2,02	1,87	4,42	2,72

1) Including possible, in part deductible income taxes at state or municipal level; source: OECD)
2) Source: IW
3) with uniform marginal tax rate of 50 % for shareholders
4) West Germany: after 1990 tax reform
5) tax burden for typical corporations; Source: OECD (1985) and Leibfritz (1987)
6) direct corporate taxation (OECD Revenue Statistics) in % of the operation surplus (= profits + interest payments) of corporated companies in the non-financial sector (own computations referring to OECD data)
7) Kay/Sen (1983) and Leibfritz (1987)
8) Leibfritz (1986)

must be considered[2]. For equipment the differences in the fiscal write-off period are kept within relatively narrow limits; in this case, varying depreciation rates result in the fact that countries like Sweden, the U.S., West Germany and Switzerland look somewhat better than Japan or the Netherlands. As countries with greater differences in the fiscal write-off period for company buildings, Italy as well as, once again, West Germany and Sweden end up relatively favorable while Japan, the Netherlands, Great Britain and (since the reform of 1988) the U.S. appear in a less favorable position.

As far as *special measures to promote investments*[3] are concerned, Austria and Sweden are the only major exceptions with their system of investment reserves; these conditions in the other countries have come to close convergence since the tax reforms in Great Britain (1984) and the U.S. (1986/88). The possibilities of *transferring losses* are most favorable in Great Britain and the U.S. and least favorable in France, Austria and Sweden. Almost every country is familiar with the possibility of transferring *undisclosed reserves* to new capital assets; however, it would be possible to establish an order here only in specific individual cases. In the *valuation of inventories*, Sweden, Great Britain, Japan and the U.S. were the most favorable in 1984. Only very little data is available for the comparison of the definition of (fiscally recognized) company expenses and the fiscal treatment of provisions and reserves; in this case, it must especially be remembered that in some countries (West Germany, Austria, Sweden and Japan) it is possible to allocate pension provisions[4].

In addition to these arrangements, there are, of course, also the manifold fiscal measures benefitting *special enterprises, industries and regions* which are interested in decisions on international direct investment; however, due to the almost endless variety of these measures, it will not be possible to take them into account here.

The available model calculations for the effective taxation on the profits of capital stock companies only partially take into account

---

2) Cf. on this and on the following *Fuest/Kroker* 1987a, *Leibfritz/Meurer* 1985 and *Leibfritz* 1987.

3) Cf. on this and on the following esp. *Leibfritz/Meurer* 1985.

4) Cf. *Leibfritz/Meurer* 1985, p. 135.

the indicated differences in the delimitation of the tax base. In most cases, the write-off conditions, the rules for the valuation of inventories and the fiscal measures to promote investments are included. To the extent that the studies were done in the early 1980's, they mostly agree in arriving at the result that the effective tax burden on the profits of "typical" capital stock companies is relatively high in West Germany, Japan and Austria, while the U.S., Great Britain, Belgium, the Netherlands, Sweden and Switzerland show lesser tax burdens; the picture does not change much if other assumptions are made on the investment behavior in the course of time or on the inflation rate[5]. Only incomplete results are available so far on the effects of the tax reforms implemented in recent years; but they indicate that the order has hardly changed[6]. In particular, the U.S. and Great Britain still seem to be among the countries with the lowest effective taxation, even after the changes in the tax laws in 1984 and 1986/88 respectively.

However, as already has been mentioned, these model calculations take only partial account of differences in the delimitation of the tax base; thus their validity is, of course, limited. Therefore, it is interesting to compare the results with *overall taxation rates* such as those resulting from the data of the OECD national accounting system. Here a comparison is made between the total of the direct company taxes actually paid and the so-called "operating surplus" (i. e., operating profit plus interest paid) of capital stock companies; assuming an identical statistical delimitation in the various countries, this indicator has the advantage that it shows the effective taxation on a comparably defined profit after any forward and backward shifting in a certain approximation. In fact, however, the available OECD data is also comparable only to a limited extent so that even the comparison of these taxation rates must be interpreted with some reservation. Based on this indicator, Japan was still among the countries with a relatively high rate of tax on profit in 1985, but Great Britain shows an even higher rate (Table 1); whereas West Germany, like the U.S., occupies a middle position here, and the tax burden in the Netherlands is particularly low[7]. The aggregate

---

5) Cf. *Leibfritz/Meurer* 1985, p. 136.

6) Cf. esp. *Leibfritz* 1987, p. 109 and *Fuest/Kroker* 1987a, p. A-11.

7) Similar calculations to those presented here can be found in *Kay/Sen* 1983 and in the OECD Economic Outlook, No. 36, 1984.

corporate tax share (corporate tax revenues as a percentage of GNP; cf. Table 1) provides a similar picture.

Regardless of the statistical inadequacies of this comparison, the divergence of the overall economic indicators from those of the model calculations are so great that a certain reticence appears in order (in relation to all results presented above) until additional computations are available. At least the possibility can not be excluded that, due to an incomplete consideration of the tax base or of the omission of possibly divergent conditions for the shifting of taxes at the international level, the results of the model calculations are to a certain degree "distorted".

The conclusion to be drawn from these considerations is that up to now there are *no really reliable data on international differences in the taxation of profits*. Nor is there any reliable knowledge as to which taxation indicators the internationally operating companies might use for their orientation. When we attempt to define the significance of profit taxation for international investment decisions later in this paper, we shall therefore have to look at differing taxation indicators.

3. Factors influencing the choice of location of international direct investments

To date there is no conclusive theory on direct investments[8]. On the basis of differing theoretical approaches, however, various motives and calculations for such investments can be deduced. To the extent that these are auxiliary commercial activities, one could fall back on the foreign trade theory. Market-orientated investments could be explained by the concept of rising returns to scale. Purchase-orientated direct investments can be explained through the use of non-availabilities. For cost-orientated foreign investments the *Ricardian* approach of comparative cost advantages may be applied. Approaches involving portfolio theories or the micro-and macroeconomic functions of investments can help in explaining international investment decisions.

---

[8] Cf. *Beyfuß* 1987, *Adebahr* 1981.

In the real world, one must assume that decisions on the location of direct investments are made on the basis of very different criteria. Above all, one must consider the following factors[9]:

- *market-orientated factors* (securing the foreign sales market, opening up new markets, circumventing import restrictions, reducing risks through distribution of the production locations);

- *cost aspects* (saving of transport costs, exploitation of advantages in costs, return and exchange rates);

- *purchasing aspects* (securing of a raw materials base, access to technologies);

- *political aspects* (taxation, regulations, political stability, investment aid).

Basically, it must be assumed that decisions concerning location are not made in accordance with an ideal or a uniform optimization model[10]. Furthermore, in view of the complexity of this decision-making process and of the frequently insufficient data basis regarding international conditions in respect to location, investment decisions also seem to be determined to a great extent by subjective assessments and expectations[11]. It is, after all, remarkable that even where a knowledge of investment accounting procedures may be taken for granted, sweeping point systems predominate in international location decisions[12]. Whether the empirical findings support the above-mentioned supposition, we will discuss later.

Figures 1 and 2 illustrate the *connection between direct investment and the mutual dependence in trade*. At least there is a clear tendency for strongly export-orientated countries to also engage to a greater degree in direct investments abroad and for countries that are more strongly import-orientated to attract direct investments from abroad to a greater degree. The fact that, in many cases, direct investments

---

9) On the following cf. esp. *Beyfuß* 1987, p. 28ff.

10) Cf. *Heigl* 1983.

11) See also *Heigl* 1983, p. 373.

12) Cf. *Heigl* 1983, p. 372 and the studies mentioned there.

Figure 1:

Outward Direct Investments and Exports of Selected Countries

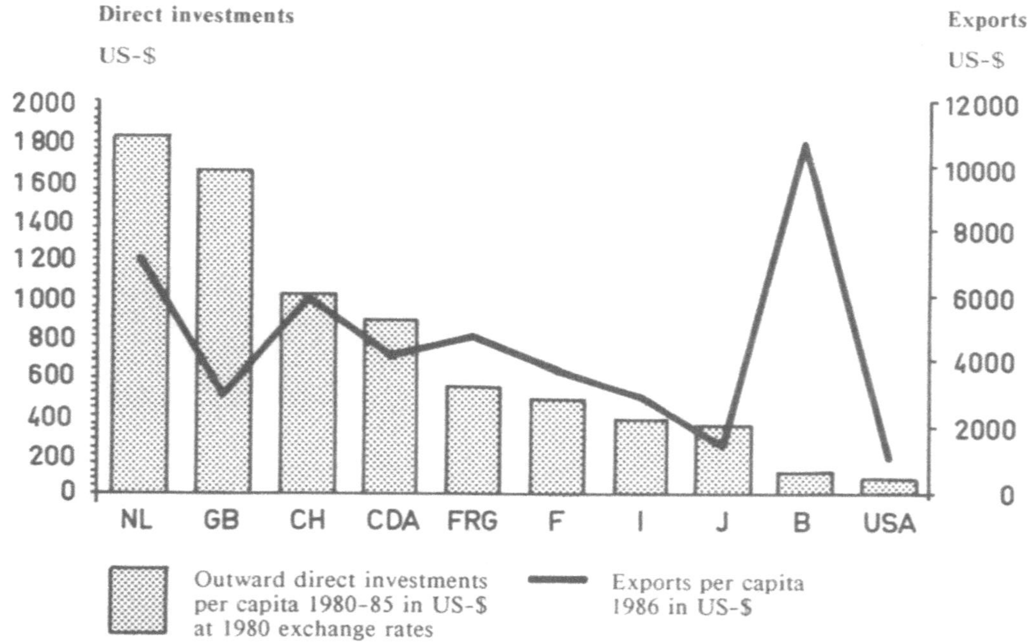

Sources: OECD, HWWA-Institute for Economic Research Hamburg, and own calculations.

Figure 2:

Inward Direct Investments in Selected Countries and Imports

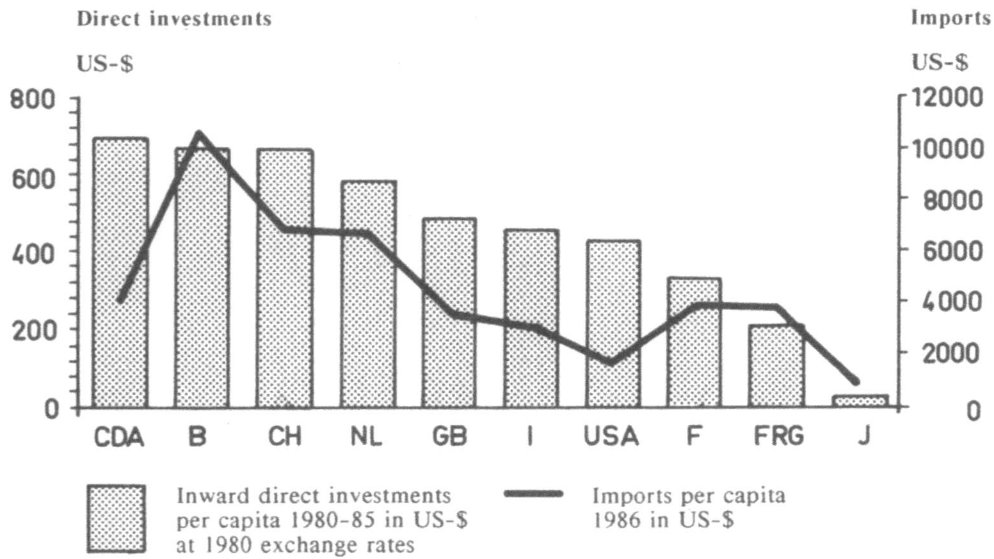

Sources: See Figure 1

run parallel to exports is also confirmed by the findings of a relatively narrowly correlated regional breakdown of West German exports and direct investments.

With the help of Figure 3, the significance of the *size of the market* for location decisions can also be indicated: Whereas the direct investments made by foreigners in the domestic market in the years 1980-1985 (calculated in constant U.S. dollar exchange rates) varied considerably from country to country, the *per capita* figures are much closer together (main exception: Japan). The coefficient of variation in the per-capita-case is much lower.

For further evidence, we will refer to some correlation computations. As the results in Tables 2 and 3 show, the significance of the other location factors (e.g. cost and political factors) appears to be less clear. There are only very few significant *correlations* which can be ascertained between the regional distribution of direct investments and individual factors in the selection of a location. This applies both to direct investments as a whole (Table 2) and especially to the foreign investments made by Japan (Table 3). Looking first at the distribution of direct investments without any per capita adjustment, above all the significance of the interdependence in foreign trade, i.e. of the parallel function of direct investments to trade, becomes visible (cf. the highly significant correlation coefficients compared with the import and/or export shares in Tables 2 and 3); in addition to this, the only significant connection is to the net return on sales (here, however, only on the basis of five countries) and in the case of Japan to (bilateral) exchange rate trends.

In order to be able to grasp the significance of the location factors on the supply side better, we may look at the per capita figures for direct investments adjusted approximately for the size of the market (Table 2). As one might expect, we do not find any significant correlation with the intensity of imports (measured as share of world imports). Here, however, one does notice the close connection with the trend and that the intensity of the fluctuations in the exchange rates is remarkable. The influence of the net return on sales has only very little significance here, while that of the gross return on investment even shows an (implausible) negative effect. The negative (although not very strong) connection to the rate of the tax burden is noteworthy.

Figure 3:

Inward Direct Investments in Selected Countries

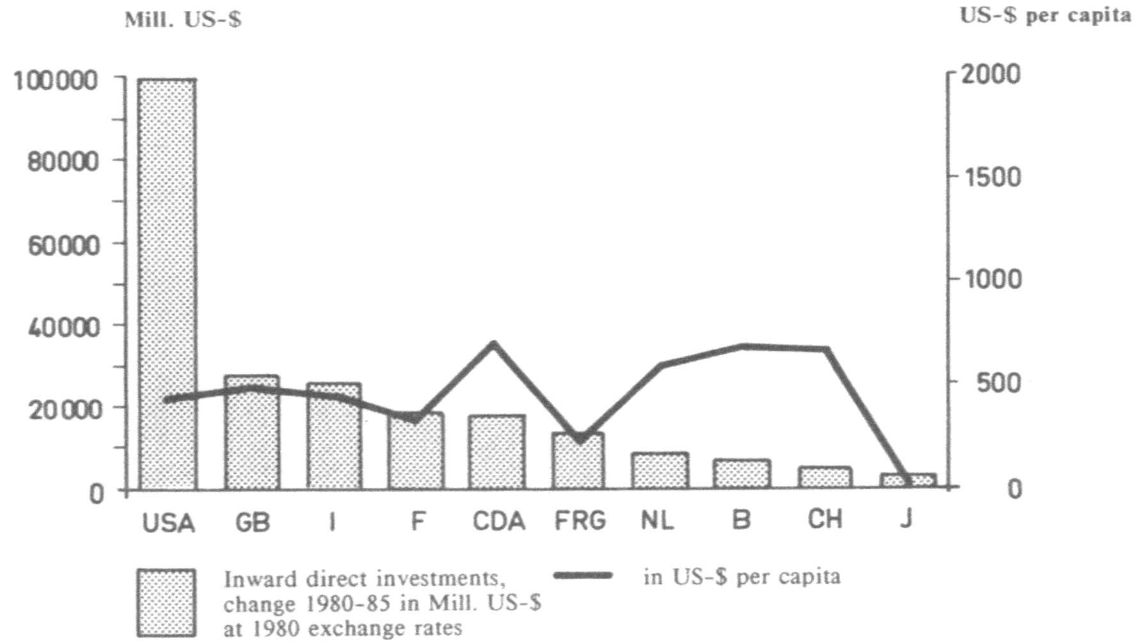

Sources: See Figure 1

Table 2:

Selected Factors Influencing the Location of International Direct Investments

	Coefficent of correlation[1]...	
	...with the distribution of foreign investments in 9 industrial countries 1980-85	...with the distribution of foreign investments per capita in 9 industrial countries 1980-85
share of world imports	0,855** (4,36)	- 0,497* (-1,51)
domestic demand[2]	0,245 (0,67)	-0,295 (-0,82)
effective exchange rates[3]	-0,083 (-0,14)	-0,687* (-1,64)
volatility of exchange rates	-0,208 (-0,37)	-0,959** (-5,82)
wage costs per unit[4]	-0,206 (-0,56)	-0,431 (-1,26)
tax burden (tariff)[5]	0,012 (0,03)	-0,729* (-2,82)
tax burden (national account)[6]	-0,182 (-0,34)	0,082 (0,17)
political stability[7]	-0,049 (-0,13)	-0,133 (-0,35)
gross return on investment[8]	-0,174 (-0,31)	-0,889** (-3,36)
net return on sales[9]	0,922** (4,12)	0,701* (1,70)

1) in brackets: t-statistic
2) average growth rates 1973-84
3) change 1975-1983
4) change 1970-1978
5) tax rate burden of incorporated companies incl. other earnings and asset taxes (IW) 1984
6) overall direct tax burden of incorporated companies (OECD national account) 1984
7) Index consisting of inflation rates, public expenditures share and deficits
8) for 5 countries (OECD)
9) for 5 countries (IW), average 1980-85

** significant with a 1 % probability of error
* significant with a 10 % probability error

Table 3:

Selected Factors Influencing the Location of Japanese Direct Investments 1975-1983

(analyzing 8 destination countries)

	Coefficient of correlation with the distribution of additional direct investments 1975-83 on 8 industrial countries
bilateral export share	0,996** (27,62)
domestic demand[2)]	0,319 (0,824)
effective exchange rate[3)]	-0,698* (-2,39)
wage costs per unit[4)]	-0,252 (-0,64)
tax burden (tariff)[5)]	0,074 (0,18)
tax burden (national account)[6)]	0,256 (0,46)
political stability[7)]	0,133 (0,33)
gross return on investment[8)]	0,534 (1,24)
net return on sales[9)]	0,866* (2,45)

1) in brackets: t-statistic
2) average growth rates 1973-84
3) change 1975-1983
4) change 1970-1978
5) tax rate burden of incorporated companies incl. other earnings and asset taxes (IW) 1984
6) overall direct tax burden of incorporated companies (OECD national account) 1984
7) Index consisting of inflation rates, public expenditures share and deficits
8) for 5 countries (OECD)
9) for 5 countries (IW)

*** significant with a 1 % probability of error
** significant with a 2.5 % probability of error
* significant with a 10 % probability of error

On the whole, these results are hardly surprising. Basically, they merely confirm that for the location of direct investments the interdependence in foreign trade and the size of the market are of primary importance. These factors are obviously overshadowed by the influences of exchange rates as well as (sales-related) profit considerations. In view of the diverging findings, the influence of taxation seems not of primary importance, but in any case the direct influence remains unclear.

Of course, this does not yet imply that the cost-related and the political factors in the choice of location are of less importance *in total*. To analyse this, we have formed an overall indicator for the "supply side" location quality of five countries (for which appropriately differentiated data are available, cf. Table 4): It contains the net return on sales (weight: 30 %), the electricity costs (10 %) and two indicators each for manpower costs and profit taxation as well as for the basic political and social conditions (weighted at 10 % each). The weighting corresponds approximately to the assessments obtained in polls taken among companies (see below for more on this). In fact, the distribution of the additional direct investments made in the period 1980-1985 among the five countries (U.S., Japan, West Germany, France and Great Britain) shows the expected positive correlation in comparison with this overall indicator for the quality of a location. Surprisingly, however, this connection is statistically highly significant only when one looks at the shares in per cent of the volume of direct investment; by contrast, if one applies the direct investments on a *per capita* basis, the result is a correlation of only little significance[13]. However, these results seem to support the above-mentioned thesis of a complex and, in some cases, sweeping decision-making process for direct investments in that the choice of location (in addition to trade- and sales-related considerations) is obviously orientated to a considerable extent to a sort of point system of evaluation of selected supply-side location factors.

Polls taken among companies engaged in business abroad take another route in identifying the significant influencing factors for

---

13) In the first case the correlation coefficient (in points) amounts to 0.857 (t = 2.89), in the second case to 0.586 (t = 1.25). The first value is significant with a probability of error of 5 %, the second only with a probability of error of 15 %.

Table 4:

Selected Indicators of the Location Quality of 5 Industrial Countries

Indicator	Weight	USA	Japan	Germany	France	UK
net return on sales, 1980-85[1)]		4,3	1,3	1,4	1,4	3,0
rank	0,3	1	5	4	3	2
strikes (number of lost working days, average 1980-85)[1)]		147,3	13,2	45,9	86,0	453,0
rank	0,1	4	1	2	3	5
electricity price ($/Kwh, 1980-85)[2)]		0,045	0,089	0,053	0,044	0,055
rank	0,1	1	5	3	1	4
real wage position (CEA, change 1960-85 in %)		1,0	-13,4	11,8	1,5	4,2
rank	0,1	2	1	5	2	3
wage costs per unit in industry 1980[4)]		0,68	0,66	0,75	0,52	0,75
rank	0,1	3	2	5	1	5
corporate income tax rates 1984[1)]		51,4	52,3	56,0	50,0	45,0
rank	0,1	3	4	5	2	1
effective tax burden on re-invested profits 1982 (Ifo)[3)]		43,6	52,9	57,5	50,5	35,4
rank	0,1	2	4	5	3	1
"political stability" (public debt, public expenditures, inflation)[5)]		1,7	5,8	1,2	-6,1	-4,4
rank	0,1	2	1	2	4	4
weighted total rank		2,0	3,3	3,9	2,5	2,9
converted in points (USA = 10)		10	6,1	5,1	8,0	6,9

1) Institute of the German Economy (IW)
2) Ministry for Commerce, North-Rhine-Westfalia
3) Leibfritz/Meurer (1985)
4) Own calculations
5) Index consisting of the reverse values of inflation rates, of the public expenditures share and the change of public deficits in % of the GNP

direct investments; such polls taken on the differences in international locations are probably less "distorted" in the political tendency than equivalent domestic polls, because economic policy consequences are hardly discussed in this case. For West German companies, especially, there are meanwhile a whole series of such polls[14]. Essentially, they confirm the above derived thesis that direct investments primarily serve to support exports, to secure markets and to open up new markets. Cost and political motives then follow, but are much less important, although the weighting is no longer uniform here; whereas in some polls political stability is given greater significance, in other polls wage costs and aspects of return play a somewhat larger role. To the extent that it is explicitly ascertained, the taxation of earnings plays a significant role, but it is still given relatively less importance among the factors named.

More recent polls indicate that in the last years factors such as political stability, favorable legislation for companies and low taxes have gained somewhat in importance[15]. As closely-knit regions move closer together politically, like the EEC for example, such differences in the quality of the supply-side conditions are likely to become somewhat more important.

4. Results and conclusions

On the whole, the empirical findings are hardly surprising: They permit the conclusion that for the choice of location for international direct investments, at least as far as investments in industrial countries are concerned, trade, sales and exchange rate orientated considerations still are the most relevant factors. In addition to this, political and cost-related factors appear to have some significance as well. But here it seems that *individual* factors such as wage costs, electricity costs, taxation or returns taken individually are not decisive; rather, in addition to the trade and market aspects, the decisions concerning location are, as is to be expected, rather orientated towards an overall view of these supply factors.

---

14) Cf. for example *Kayser* et al. 1980, *Pfeil* 1981 as well as the studies cited in *Deitmars* 1982 and *Heigl* 1983.

15) Cf. Industriemagazin 1987.

As far as the specific role of profit taxation is concerned, our findings - and this corresponds with the result just explained - do not permit any clear conclusions. Whereas the significant correlation between (per capita) direct investment and the rate of tax on profits in our comparison of nine countries argues for a stronger influence, the other correlation values named as well as the results of the company polls rather point in the opposite direction. Our calculations might be interpreted in such a way that, to the extent that tax considerations are relevant at all, the generally more familiar standard tax rates have a greater influence on the location decisions than the effective tax burden. This hypothesis would be compatible with the finding mentioned earlier on that, in making their decisions regarding locations, the companies frequently go by relatively simple, and to a certain extent also subjective, point systems of evaluation. However, more detailed studies would have to determine whether this thesis is really correct. If it is correct, a possible measure of a policy aimed at improving the quality of domestic locations would be to reduce the tax rates on profits while at the same time broadening the tax base. Such a strategy, by the way, would also be compatible with demands for a fiscal system of so-called "broad-based taxes".

References

Adebahr, H., Direktinvestitionen, Berlin 1981

Beyfuß, J., Direktinvestitionen im Ausland, Köln 1987

Deitmers, J., Auslandsinvestitionen und inländische Beschäftigung, Frankfurt/Bern 1982

Fuest, W./*Kroker*, R., Unternehmens- und Investitionsbesteuerung im internationalen Vergleich, in: IW-Trends, No. 1, 1987, pp. A1-A17 (1987a)

Fuest, W./*Kroker*, R., Einkommensbesteuerung in zehn Industrieländern, in: IW-Trends, No. 2, 1987, pp. B1-B13 (1987b)

Fuest, W./*Kroker*, R., Neutralität der Unternehmensbesteuerung und investive Standortqualität, in: IW-Trends, Heft 4, 1987, pp. A1-A8 (1987c)

Heigl, A., Betriebswirtschaftliche Bedingungen für fiskalische Standortanreize bei grenzüberschreitender Unternehmenstätigkeit, in: L. *Fischer* (ed.), Unternehmung und Steuer, Festschrift für P. *Scherpf*, Wiesbaden 1983, pp. 363-374

Kay, J./*Sen*, J., The Comparative Burden of Business Taxation, IFS Working Paper No. 45, London 1983

Kayser, G., et al., Erfahrungen deutscher Auslandsinvestoren in ausgewählten Industrieländern, Göttingen 1980

Leibfritz, W., Steuerliche Belastung und staatliche Förderung der Kapitalbildung in der Bundesrepublik Deutschland, Ifo-Institut für Wirtschaftsforschung, München 1986

Leibfritz, W., Die Unternehmensbesteuerung im internationalen Vergleich, in: Steuern und wirtschaftliche Entwicklung, Beihefte zur Konjunkturpolitik, Berlin 1987

Leibfritz, W./*Meurer*, C., Steuerliche Investitionsförderung im internationalen Vergleich, Berlin/München 1985

OECD, Revenue Statistics of OECD Member Countries 1965-1986, Paris 1986

Wenn das Klima stimmt, in: Industriemagazin, July 1987, (no author given), pp. 135-139

Segregation between Long-term and Short-term Finance
- A Topic Concerning Financial Liberalization in Japan -

Tsuyoshi Kanegae

1. Introduction

The post-war financial system of Japan has had three major characteristics: a) the regulation of interest rates including the adoption of "intentionally lower interest rate policy"; b) the regulation of business lines of various financial institutions; and c) the isolation of the domestic economy from overseas countries by restricting foreign exchange and capital transactions.

Almost all of these regulations, formed in the 1950's after World War II, performed well during the past period of fast economic growth, by contributing to the efficient allocation of scarce funds when the demand for funds expanded rapidly.

In the 1980's as the Japanese economy entered a stage of stable growth, and became what has been called an "Economic Giant", the above-mentioned characteristics have turned out to be rather obsolete and a deterrent to the economy. These characteristics have been criticized both inside and outside of Japan.

Naturally, the authorities have gradually changed their policies. Since the oil crisis, they have accelerated the so-called "Liberalization and Internationalization of Finance". The factors most influential to these changes were: a) internally, the large-scale floating of government bonds to cope with the recession caused by the oil crisis; b) externally, the 1983 summit talks between Japan and the United States on the yen-U.S. dollar problem.

Consequently, the govenment had to take measures such as adding some advantages to government bonds. One such measure was the issuance of new types of bonds bearing more flexible yields than before; another measure was to increase the number of maturity dates for various types of short and medium-term bonds (from 6 months to 5 years). The government also had to ease regulation of the various rates of interest in accordance with these measures. They also liberalized foreign exchange transactions, by revising the Foreign Exchange and Foreign Trade Control Law in 1980.

The authorities were also forced to deregulate the business lines of various financial institutions. An example is the segregation system between the banking and securities businesses. In April of 1983, the banks were first allowed to carry out subscription activities of long-term (10 years) government bonds as well as local government bonds and government-guaranteed bonds. In June of 1984, the banks were allowed to deal (buying and selling) in the above three kinds of public bonds in the market. This deregulation was realized by reforming the "Securities Exchange Law of 1947" which had severely prohibited the banks from engaging in securities business, and by the revision of the "Banking Law of 1927", in 1981.

Deregulation of the business fields of various financial institutions has been continuously under consideration. In December of 1987, the Committee on Financial System Research submitted a report titled, "How the Specialized Financial Institutions should be". In February of 1988, a sub-committee was organized to discuss more detailed and concrete policy measures.

In this study, we will try to analyze one aspect of the second characteristic of the Japanese financial system, namely, the segregation between long-term and short-term finance. In this paper, we use the words "long-term finance" to indicate financial instruments with the maturity date of more than one year, and "short-term finance" to indicate financial instruments with a maturity date of less than one year.

Also, the term "segregation system between the long-term and short-term finance" is defined as the system which prohibits banks from concurrently engaging in both long and short-term deposits, loans and other finance businesses. However, we will not go further into any problems of the segregation system which concern the securities business and trust business, despite the fact that these are also of a long-term nature.

This study will proceed as follows:

(1) First of all, we take a retrospective look at the historical background of the segregation system by looking at the establishment of "special banks" for specific purposes, and at the establishment of long-term credit banks under the special laws.

(2) Next, we emphasize the theoretical background for the system by examining the so-called "Commercial Banking Principle" which has been adopted in Japan since the Meiji Era.

(3) After this, we briefly overview the systems of long-term finance in western developed countries.

(4) Fourthly, we analyze the present condition of the segregation system in Japan. This is done by pointing out problems the system has caused in the actual banking operations of the long-term credit banks and the ordinary banks ("City Banks" and "Regional Banks").

(5) Fifthly, we look into the controversy regarding the merits and demerits of the segregation system, along with the discussions of the Committee on Financial System Research.

(6) Finally, recognizing the changing financial environment, we analyze the prospects of the segregation system, in search of a better system for the national economy.

2. Historical background of the segregation system - An analysis of the traditional system of specialized financial institutions in Japan

2.1. The establishment of "special banks" for long-term credit

The idea of the segregation system in Japan is fundamentally based on the "Commercial Banking Principle". This principle was historically observed in a document[1] written in 1882 when the Bank of Japan was founded. In the document, it was emphasized that the central bank was not to deal with long-term funds for agriculture or manufacture, but was only to finance commercial transactions. In this context, the Bank of Japan itself was a sort of commercial bank.

---

[1] The document is the prospectus of the Bank of Japan; see Bank of Japan 1986.

From this point of view, "Special Banks" were set up under special laws passed during the years 1897 to 1902, as the long-term credit banks providing financing for agriculture or other long-term funds. These were: Japan Hypothec Bank (Nihon Kangyo Bank), Agriculture and Manufacture Banks (Noko Bank, one bank in each prefecture), Hokkaido Colonial Bank (Takushoku Bank), Japan Industrial Bank (Nihon Kogyo Bank) and so on[2].

They operated in this capacity until the General Headquarters of Allied Forces (G. H. Q.) ordered them to close or to transform themselves into "ordinary banks". This was done in the name of the democratization process and because of the general view that long-term funds should be raised in the capital market. Thus, in 1948, Nihon Kangyo Bank and Hokkaido Takushoku Bank, converted into the ordinary banks respectively. In 1950, Nihon Kogyo Bank also converted into an ordinary bank.

2.2. The system of the long-term credit banks

In this way, for some time after World War II, the ordinary banks played the role of supplying both long-term and short-term funds. On the other hand, since the capital market was not yet sufficiently developed, the ordinary banks had to carry the burden of the so-called "Over-Loan Phenomenon"[3].

In December of 1951, the Ministry of Finance asked the Temporary Conference on the Financial System to discuss the establishment of long-term financial institutions. In the next year, the law for the long-term credit banks was enacted.

The first to obey this law was The Japan Industrial Bank which changed to a long-term credit bank (hereafter LTCB) from an ordinary bank. Following this, The Japan Long-term Credit Bank, a new bank, was set up, obtaining long-term business from Nihon

---

[2] The Bank of Korea and the Bank of Taiwan (closed in 1945), Yokohama Specie Bank (changed to an ordinary bank in 1947 and again shifted to the specialized foreign exchange bank, "The Bank of Tokyo" in 1954).

[3] The word "over-loan" is a Japanese-English term frequently used in financial circles during a period of a rapid economic growth. It has no clear definition but describes the situation where (a) banks' loans constantly exceed their deposits, and (b) the deficits are made up by borrowing from the Bank of Japan (see *Suzuki* 1985).

Kangyo Bank and Hokkaido Takushoki Bank. And then, in 1957, Nihon Real Estate Bank (renamed to Nihon Saiken Shin-yo Bank in 1977) was founded.

According to the Long-term Credit Bank Law, the LTCBs are the banks licensed by the Ministry of Finance under the LTCBs Law. They are not prescribed in the "Bank Law". The main characteristics of the LTCBs are as follows: a) LTCBs are banks specializing in long-term finance. It was hoped they would help lighten the burden of "over-loan" being borne by the ordinary banks; b) LTCBs are authorized to issue bank debentures to raise funds up to 30 times their combined total of capital and reserves. They are not allowed to accept deposits from anybody other than qualified customers who are listed by the law; c) LTCBs have fewer branches than ordinary banks as they raise funds mainly by issuing bank debentures; d) Their security investment business and entrustment business are recognized as their primary business, while those of ordinary banks are regarded as their secondary business.

3. Theoretical background of the segregation system - "Commercial banking principle" -

The commercial banking principle is, as noted, the principle of the banking business which was established in England in the nineteenth century. At this time, England's banking system had already been developed. In the middle of 19th century, it was said that British banks were too busy supplying working funds to commerce, and had no room for long-term finance.

The Japanese banking system, built in the early years of the Meiji Era, followed the British banking system. So, as a matter of course, the principle was also imported at the same time. The principle has been generally supported in Japan, and this may have been the main reason the government kept the segregation policy for so long after World War II.

The commercial banking principle rests on the notion that, since the funds of commercial or deposit banks principally depend upon short-term deposits with higher liquidity, the funds should be invested into short-term assets such as commercial discount papers which are paid back by the merchant when he sells goods. What is more, according to the principle, the investment to the manufacturing industries must correspond to, or match with, funds raised with longer maturity dates, because the investment is of a long-term nature.

There exists some criticism against the "commercial banking principle". One is made by J. G. *Gurley* and E. S. *Shaw*. As they did not recognize any essential differences between commercial banks and the others, they naturally did not agree with the principle. There is another view which has recently been advocated in Japan among academic circles[4]. This view depends on the principle of "Economies of Scope". The principle states that, in the case of banking business, banks might hold much information which is not resalable but which is useful in many ways. The diversified operation is more efficient for banks than the system of the so-called single-product or that of "division of labor".

Another point of the discussions relates to the "Commercial Banking Principle" (the so-called "Universal Banking System"), which allows banks to operate both banking and securities businesses. The system is, as is well-known, adopted in western European countries like West Germany, France, and Switzerland. It is not adopted in the United States or Japan.

The "Universal Banking System" is a system which allows banks to operate in the securities business or in the securities investment trust business as well as in the banking business. Since this includes many interesting problems, we regret that we have no space to discuss it here.

4. Brief overview of the systems in western developed countries

The following is a brief overview of the systems of long-term and short-term finance in the main industrialized countries (i.e., Italy, France, England, West Germany and The United States). Among these five, only Italy and France adopted the segregation system. This system continued until the 1970's. The other three countries did not adopt this system, despite the fact that specialized financial institutions for medium and long-term finance exist.

---

[4] See *Tachi* 1986 and *Miyazawa* 1988.
Prof. K. *Miyazawa* insisted that one of the factors promoting the recent development of the information net-work society, was "Economies of Scope". However, the role of "Economies of Net-work" was also important (see *Miyazawa* 1988).

4.1. Italy

In Italy the fence between short-term financial institutions (commercial banks) and medium or long-term financial institutions was built under the Bank Law of 1938. This was one of the measures encacted to solve the financial crisis of around 1930. The Italian Industrial Bank was the special bank[5] for long-term finance with half of its shares owned by the government. The bank raised its funds by both deposits, and by debentures with a maturity date of more than 18 months. This allowed them to extend loans of more than 18 months, while the short-term financial institutions (commercial banks etc.) were not allowed to accept deposits and extend loans of more than 18 months.

However, since 1980, the regulations have been eased for the purpose of promoting the principle of competition. In 1972, the commercial banks were authorized to extend loans up to 5 years. However, long-term loans can comprise not more than 25 % of the lending portfolio. In May of 1985, the Council of the Cabinet Ministers on Credit decided to further ease the regulations, and now concrete plans are being examined by the Bank of Italy, which is the country's central bank[6].

4.2. France

In France the principle of segregation between long-term and short-term finance was established under the Bank Law of 1945. Banks were divided into three groups: the deposit banks, the industrial banks and the medium or long-term credit banks. The deposit banks are the only banks that can accept deposits and extend loans with a maturity date of less than two years. The industrial banks are, in other words, specialized banks for long-term credit, investing and promoting enterprises with their own capital or with funds borrowed from other banks. They are prohibited from accepting deposits and making loans for less than two year time periods. Medium or long-

---

[5] As there is a "Central Bank for Medium-Term Credit to Small Business Firms", another special organization, and concerning private institutions, there are the "Medium-Term Credit Bank" and the "Industrial Finance Company".

[6] For further detail regarding the situation in Europe and the U.S., see Kin-yu Seido Chousakai 1969 and Kin-yu Zaisei Jijo Kenkyukai 1988.

term credit banks resemble industrial banks but they can issue debentures to raise funds, and they can supply long-term loans for capital investments[7].

The new Bank Law, partly revised in 1966, eased the regulations between deposit banks and industrial banks, and made it possible for deposit banks to provide financing of more than two years. After 1984 when the Law for Activities and Superintendencies of the Financial Institutions was enacted, the classification between banks mentioned above was abolished. This was done to reflect changes in actual banking practices, and for the purpose of promoting competition among banks. Now, in France, the segregation system no longer exists.

4.3. England

In England no regulations exist regarding the terms of finance by banks, although "Clearing Banks" have traditionally followed the commercial banking principle. However, after World War II, specialized financial institutions for long-term credit were set up to cope with the needs of basic industries, and the shortage of capital for small business firms. They are, Finance Corp. Industry Ltd., Industrial and Commercial Finance Corp.Ltd., and Building Societies. FIC, set up in 1945, extends long-term loans of 7 to 10 years to key industries. ICFC raises funds by issuing bonds with a maturity date of 20 to 30 years. It also supplies funds for small enterprises. Building Societies are, where it is noted, private financial institutions for "housing loans". They were first founded in 1850.

Clearing Banks are also transforming their funding operations, adopting time-deposits of seven years and expanding their business to consumer loans or "term-loans".

4.4. West Germany

In West Germany, there is no boundary between the banking business and securities business, or between long-term and short-

---

7) The special banks for long-term credit, first set up in Japan in the Meiji Era, reportedly followed after Credit Foncier, and the ideas of special banks and bank debentures in Japan also have French origins (see Federation . . . 1984).

term finance since the "Universal Banking System" has been adopted. However, the following rule is in effect for the purpose of matching the terms of sources and uses of funds: The aggregate amount of long-term loans, unlisted stocks and bonds, and movables or real estates, with a period of more than four years, can not exceed the total amount of 10 % of the funds of four years term, plus 60 % of savings deposits, plus the outstanding short-term bank debentures, plus the long-term bank debentures, plus the equity capital.

As for the specialized financial institutions for long-term credit, there are: Kreditanstalt für Wiederaufbau (KfW), Industrie-Kreditbank AG (IKB), and Realkreditinstitute (RKI). The KfW is a government-related financial institution founded with the funds of the Marshall Plan in 1948. IKB is a private institution for long-term finance to medium or small-sized business firms. RKI consists both of private and government-owned institutions, and supplies long-term funds by issuing bonds.

4.5. The United States

In the United States, there is no fence between the long-term and short-term finance business of the banks. However, there is segregation between the banking business and the securities business under the *Glass-Steagall* Act (The Banking Act of 1933)[8]. As for specialized financial institutions for medium and long-term finance, The Federal Land Bank and Federal Intermediate Credit Banks are for agricultural financing and are government-related organizations, while Savings and Loans Associations, and Mutual Saving Banks are institutions for house mortgages.

5. Present situation of the segregation system in Japan - The problems in the banking practices

Now, we would like to analyze the problems caused by the segregation system for the actual banking operations of both the long-term credit banks and the ordinary banks. The problems can be

---

[8] On March 2 of 1988, the Banking Committee of the Upper House passed a bill called the "Finance Modernization Act" which, if passed, would amend the *Glass-Steagall* Act, and allow a bank holding company to hold a securities company as a subsidiary, and authorize the security company to hold shares of a finance company, which would also be subsidiary.

classified into two groups: the sources and the uses of funds. In the case of the use of funds, we wish to point out the fact that the similarity of the two types of banks has been promoted, despite the intentions of the policy. And in the case of the sources of funds, because of the difficulty of raising long-term funds, the ordinary banks are suffering from the imbalance between the long-term nature of the uses and the short-term nature of the sources of funds.

5.1. The increased similarity of the two types of banks

In the ordinary banks, the proportion of long-term loans to total loans has increased, while in the long-term credit banks the proportion of long-term loans has decreased. The share of long-term loans of the city banks, one class of the ordinary banks, was only 5 % as of the end of fiscal year (FY) 1955.

However, at the end of FY 1985, that figure increased to 35 %. On the other hand, the proportion of long-term loans in the LTCBs was 87 % in FY 1955 with the rate decreasing to 73 % in FY 1985. Consequently, the role of the ordinary banks in supplying long-term funds became large, while, the character of the LTCBs changed (now they might be called as "Short-Term & LTCBs").

What were the reasons for these changes? We can point out the following four: a) There have been no regulations or controls on the long-term loans of the ordinary banks. Even if the authorities would have formally regulated the long-term loans, the banks could have supplied the long-term funds on customer's demand by revolving or revising the short-term loans. b) During the period of fast economic growth, the demand for long-term funds was so large that the ordinary banks were led to participate in the syndicated group for the long-term loans organized by the LTCBs. c) The third reason observed is a change in the lending activity of the ordinary banks. In the ordinary banks, the need for long-term funds increased as they increased loans to the medium or small-sized firms who were not customers of the LTCBs, and also as they increased housing loans to individuals. d) As a reason for the decrease of the long-term loans in the LTCBs, we can point out the fact that the large scale enterprises in the manufacturing industry, who have been the main customers of the LTCBs, decreased their demand for funds. This was the result of a slow-down of capital investment and a strengthening of their own ability to finance projects.

5.2. The imbalance between the terms of sources and uses of funds

The businesses of the LTCBs and the ordinary banks were formally separated from each other by the Bank Law and the Law of LTCBs respectively. However, as we mentioned above, there were no regulations on the long-term loans of ordinary banks. There were also no strict controls on the operation of the short-term business of the LTCBs (i.e. deposits or short-term loans) since many exceptional articles and clauses were included in the Law of LTCBs. Therefore, the main difference between the two types of banks were the restrictions ordinary banks faced in raising long-term funds. This is the prohibition, to the ordinary banks, of issuing bank debentures and accepting medium or long-term deposits.[9]

Consequently, in the ordinary banks, an imbalance between the terms of sources and uses of funds was brought about. This trend was accelerated when the deregulations of interest rates caused an increase in the number of short-term deposit instruments bearing floating rates. The imbalance, that is to say, the "mismatching" of the terms in the assets and liabilities is of primary concern, since this is an obstacle for further development of the long-term business in ordinary banks. Furthermore, it is a factor of increased management-risk in the process of deregulation of interest rates.

6. Controversies on the merits and demerits of the segregation system - Discussions at the Committee on Financial System Research

6.1. Background factors of the controversies

The controversy on the segregation system was started by the city banks in the middle of the 1960's. They insisted that the LTCBs would soon become unnecessary, because of the slow-down trend in capital investment and in the economy as a whole, and that even the city banks could meet the demand for the long-term funds, if they were authorized to accept medium-term deposits. However, the real intention seemed to be to complain about the underwriting of the

---

9) Recently, a gradual deregulation has taken place. During the decade from 1971 to 1981, Ordinary Banks were authorized to accept time deposits with the maturity of longer than one year (now, 2 years time deposits exist with a maturity date that can be designated up to 3 years). In 1985, Ordinary Banks were first allowed to float convertible bonds in foreign currency provided the funds were used to finance equipment expenditures.

debentures issued by the LTCBs under the circumstances of a shortage of funds.

Again, at the end of the 1970's, the segregation system was challenged, when the city banks requested longer term deposits as a countermeasure for the fund-shift from the deposit banks to the LTCBs or the trust banks. The shift was caused by the introduction of new financial assets[10] bearing higher interest rates than those of deposit banks.

In the middle of the 1980's, the controversy over the system became more active than ever before because of the following changes and developments in the Japanese economy: a) The first factor was a change in the flow of funds (money-flow). The decrease in the shortage of funds for the corporate business sector has been most prominent. This was caused by a slow-down of capital expenditures. Furthermore, the so-called "over-loan" phenomenon has almost disappeared. This has been one of the main reasons for the existence of the LTCBs; b) The second factor was the progress of "Financial Liberalization" in this country. This consisted of the deregulation of interest rates and of the business lines of various financial institutions.

6.2. The reports of the Committee of Financial System Research

The Committee has shown its opinions on this matter in reports submitted four times in the past. We can regard these opinions as the views of the government, since the Ministry of Finance usually has taken the measures according to contents of the reports. It is clear that the first two reports are quite different from the latter two, and the following is an outline of each of the four reports.

a) The report of 1970 ("What should the general private financial institutions be?")

The report supported the segregation system and was highly supportive of the role of the LTCBs due to their expertise and

---

10) For instance, there are the so-called "BIG" and "WIDE". The former is a kind of loan trust, and the dividend is only paid at the maturity date after 5 years. The latter is a sort of bank debenture and the interest is only paid at the maturity date after 5 years. The dividend is re-invested, and the interest is calculated by a compound method.

neutrality. (However, under the report, time-deposits of a year and a half were authorized for the ordinary banks in 1971. This was succeeded by a "2 year time-deposit", which was introduced in 1974.)

b) The report of 1974 ("The prospects of ordinary banks and the reform of the Bank Law")

In this report the segregation system was again supported. It was thought that the LTCBs had played a major role in reforming the industrial structure of Japan and that they had contributed to the large scale projects such as the development of natural resources. (Under this report, the limit for bank debentures was expanded from 20 to 30 times of the combined total of the capital and reserves of the banks).

c) The report of 1985 ("The progress in financial liberalization and the adjustment of its environments")

For the first time, the report mentioned that the time had come to review the segregation system, because of the development of financial internationalization and the deregulation of interest rates. It also stated that it was important for banks to take into consideration "term-matching" between the sources and uses of funds. (Under the report, in the fall of 1985, the Special Research Association, as a subordinate organization of the Committee, was set up to investigate the specialized financial institutions.)

d) The report of 1987 ("What should the specialized financial institutions be?")

In the report, the various problems of specialized financial institutions were investigated. The report concluded that it was necessary to reform the financial system to meet the changes in the environment, and suggested the prospects of each type of specialized institution.

Concerning the LTCBs, the report did not have a clear opinion, but mentioned that the segregation system should be reviewed at this stage since no other developed countries have adopted the segregation system practiced in this country. The report also admitted the similarity between the ordinary banks and the LTCBs, and the existence of "mismatching" in the fund-operation of ordinary banks. It also suggested that ordinary banks should investigate alternative means of raising long-term funds and the expansion of the scope of the securities business in the LTCBs. These problems are to be discussed more specifically at the special committee just started in February of this year.

6.3. Opinions of the ordinary banks and the LTCBs

a) The opinion of the city banks[11]: The witnesses of the city banks testified to the sub-committee as follows: Firstly, the similarity of LTCB's and city banks has been developed both in domestic and overseas markets; secondly, since they have been restricted in raising long-term funds, "mismatching" was brought about with long-term assets, and this would become an obstacle for banking operations under the floating system of interest rates; thirdly, the restriction on raising long-term funds have caused a prominent handicap for the city banks in the overseas market.

The witnesses also mentioned that it was necessary to discontinue the segregation system, since its historical role had come to an end. They also believed that the financial institutions should have made an effort to improve their services and efficiency under the free market. They asked the government to approve medium-term deposits, the floating of debentures and other bonds[12] both outside and inside of the country, and the means of "securitizations" or "liquidations" of loans extended to the customers.

b) The opinion of the LTCBs: The witnesses for the LTCBs argued that the ordinary banks should have strictly followed the commercial banking principle and it was not preferable to invest or fix funds in long-term assets, since the deposits were the core of the payment system of the national economy. They also insisted that the banking system of the country should not follow the practices in other countries.

As for the roles and the prospects of the LTCBs, they stated that they played an important role in industrial finance because of their expertise and neutrality. These characteristics were, they insisted, fully supported by the segregation system.

---

11) See Kin-yu Taisei Jijo Kenkyukai 1988.

12) Includes bonds with warrant, subordinate debentures, etc.

They expect they will become "whole-sale banks"[13] with international business. In order to reach their aim, they requested the government to allow them to underwrite private bonds and to enter the trust business which, up to this time, has been restricted to security companies and trust banks.

7. Prospects of the segregation system in search of a better system for the national economy (conclusions)

In this paper, we have discussed the historical and theoretical backgrounds, the situation of foreign countries, the present situation and problems, as well as the controversies, concerning the segregation system between long-term and short-term finance.

7.1. The summary of the study

a) The LTCBs were set up under special circumstances of the economy after World War II. They were designated to be specialized financial institutions to supplement long-term finance, and to lighten the burden of the so-called "over loan" of the ordinary banks.

b) The system was theoretically based on what we call the "Commercial Banking Principle". However, there have been debates whether or not the banks should have followed this principle, and recently, the interesting ideas of "economies of scope" or "economies of net-work" have been advocated as new notions concerning business fields of the enterprises. The "Universal Banking System" is another important theme to be discussed.

c) The survey of the systems of other developed countries shows that only a few countries adopted the segregation system, and even in those countries, the trend was to ease regulations in order to promote efficiency in the banking business by free competition.

d) Regarding the practice of actual banking operations, the ordinary banks became more like the long-term credit banks and the LTCBs increased their short-term business. This phenomenon is

---

13) In general, a "whole-sale bank" is a bank engaging in the underwriting or brokerage business of securities, M & A, etc., in addition to the banking business, and raising funds from money market.

essentially based on the imbalance of the regulations, and the trends were accelerated by the structural changes in the economy and the flow of funds.

e) In their report, the majority of the members of the Committee on Financial System Research recognized the following: If the authorities continue to develop "Financial Liberalization", they would inevitably come across the barriers, e.g., the system of specialized financial institutions; and the most important problem there, is the regulations on the floating of bank debentures.

7.2. Conclusions

a) Judging from the structural changes in both the Japanese economy and in financial transactions, and also from the present situation observed in banking practices, we come to the conclusion that the segregation system has already finished the role it occupied for nearly forty years after World War II. And we agree with the opinions of the Committee that it is necessary for us to improve the financial systems as time goes by.

b) We believe that the trend of "Financial Liberalization and Internationalization" will inevitably be followed by reforms of the segregation system in various fields. This will happen because deregulation of interest rates can not be further promoted without the reconstruction of a new financial system.

c) When developing a reform plan for a new system, it is important to remember that we must consider the prospects of the LTCBs. The LTCBs will become, what we call, "Whole-sale Banks", engaging in both the securities business and international business. Considering the results realized in the past in the domestic and foreign security market, something should be done about the restrictions on the acceptable deposits and the numbers of branch offices of LTCBs. This is also what the LTCBs expect. Therefore, it is necessary for the government to take these steps in order to bring about the desired results.

d) On the other hand, it is necessary to adopt measures which permit ordinary banks to issue bank debentures and utilize other means of raising long-term funds.

e) As a result of these steps, the segregation system will be substantially abolished and the desirable transformations of the two types of banks will be promoted. Further competition between the two types of banks will increase the efficiency of the banking administration. The banks must prepare themselves for new steps in their future.

f) We wish to make a final comment on the idea of "Investment Banks"[14], which has been raised in the latest report of the Committee. We should consider carefully whether or not such a new kind of bank is necessary to meet the needs of the customers. Desirable financial systems are built for the benefit of the national economy as a whole, and not for the interest of the financial institutions. It is not clear if the concept of an "Investment Bank" would benefit the system as a whole.

---

14) There is no clear definition for "investment bank", but what the committee meant is the bank specialized in whole-sale banking business and securities business as the subsidiary or affiliated company of the banks or security companies.

References

Bank of Japan, Wagakuni no Kin-yu Seido (Financial System in Japan), Tokyo (Nihon Shin-yo Chosa Co., Ltd.) 1986

Federation of Bankers Association of Japan, Banking System in Japan, Tokyo (Zenginkyo) 1984

Kanegae, T., Besonderheiten der Geldvermögensbildung in Japan, Beihefte zu Kredit und Kapital, Berlin 1985

Kanegae, T., Outline of Japanese Financial Institutions and the Characteristics, in: Chushokigyo Kenkyu, No. 8, Chukyo University, (Nagoya) 1986

Kin-yu Seido Chousakai, Choki Kin-yu Seido (Long-term Credit Bank System), Tokyo (Kin-yu Zaisei Jijo Kenkyukai) 1969

Kin-yu Zaisei Jijo Kenkyukai, Senmon Kin-yu Kikan Seido ni Tsuite (On the Specialized Financial Institutions), Tokyo (Kinzai) 1988

Miyazawa, K., Gyosaika to Johoka (Deregulations of Operations and Network of Information in the Industry), Tokyo (Yuhikaku) 1988

Senda, J./*Kanegae*, T./*Okuno*, H., Henkakuki no Ginko to Shoken (Banking and Securities Business in the Reforming Period), Tokyo (Yuhikaku) 1986

Suzuki, Y., Kin-yu Juyuka to Kin-yu Seisaku (Deregulations in Finance and Monetary Policy), Tokyo (Toyo Keizai Shinposha) 1985

Suzuki, Y., Financial Reform in Japan - Development and Prospects, Monetary and Economic Studies, The Bank of Japan, Vol. 5, No. 3, Dec., Tokyo 1987

Tachi, R., Kin-yu Saihensei no Shiten (Viewpoints of Financial Restructuring in Japan), Tokyo (Toyo Keizai Shinposha) 1986

On the Connection Between Economy and Ecology in International Economic Relations

Theodor Dams

1. The old issue of welfare economics

Within the framework of market economies, world trade must be reconsidered as an "extended" version of internal competition between microeconomic units on an international level. Subsequently, the theoretical welfare considerations on the domestic market need to be transferred to international economic relations. At this point, the potential for and the importance of the conflict between two welfare functions becomes obvious:

(1) Welfare of the respective country (under the different preconditions of free trade, protectionism, optimal tariffs, etc.).

(2) Conceptions of a "Global Welfare" (aggregation of values of individual countries - respectively the derivative of the goals of a "Global Society"). Whoever adheres to the concept of the international divison of labor in theory, will soon recognize the limits of welfare economics. Such limits are described by their negligible efficiency and reality in terms of practical economic policy.

In order to attain both (1) and (2), the marginal costs of two goods exchanged internationally need to be equal, and the marginal social costs on the international level should not deviate from the marginal private costs. The issue of normative economics becomes even more apparent when all of these conditions (among others, the income distribution) are included in the assessment of international economic relations.

2. The new dimension in the ecological issue

Nevertheless, these *general* limitations of welfare economics are not to imply that better explanations are to be found in special aspects by enlarging the knowledge of external effects in international economic relations. The objective of this paper is to show the connection between economy and ecology in international economic relations by examining several partial aspects. Based on the results of these partial approaches, alternatives for decision-making in international economic policy are derived due to the fact that we do not have an overall, accepted welfare function on the national or international level. Altogether, a comprehensive analysis should include the positive (e.g., *Haberler*'s productivity theory of international trade) as well as the negative external effects (e.g., trans-border pollution).

3. Classification of external effects

In Figure 1, the relationship between "Those Affected" and "Those Causing" is systematically analyzed, using the four entities for GNP-accounting, namely; "Enterprises", "Private Households", "State/Government", and "Foreign Countries".

The blank rectangles represent interdependences of non-market relations within a society. For external effects which link together foreign countries, the squares are lightly shaded. Finally, there is an area where neither national entities nor individual countries are directly responsible (dark space, Figure 1). In the latter case, both have the opportunity to lower their production costs by "exporting" external diseconomies (i.e., polluted air and water) to international public territories (oceans, atmosphere, etc.). Foreign countries and territories not claimed by any state are more or less located outside of the realms of any national economic and social accounting. Nevertheless, neighboring countries take a stand against production activities of individual states which negatively influence the living conditions or seriously weaken their own international competitive position (e.g., Rhine River problems between Switzerland, France, W. Germany, and the Netherlands). Solutions are less tangible for far reaching areas (oceans, the atmosphere, etc.) where no country or respective entity can be held accountable for damages or negative impacts of such external diseconomies. Based on these general reflections, the topics "Economy" and "Ecology" cover at least two problems in international relations:

Figure 1:
Causing and Affected Parties in the National and International Context

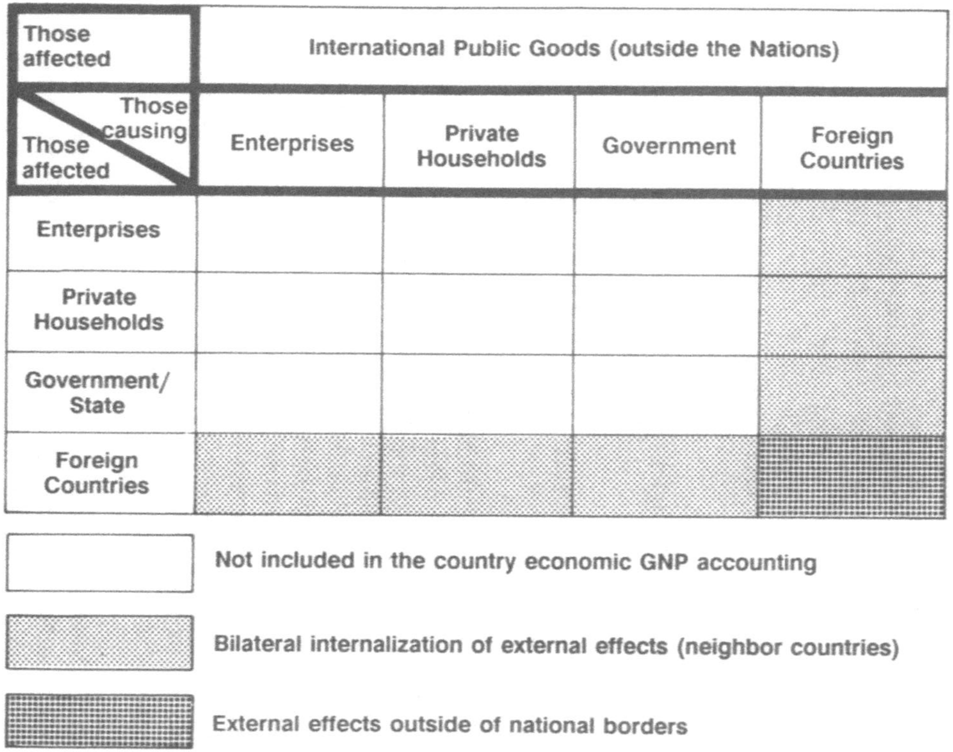

(1) Companies, households, and governments (states) can pass on a part of their costs to neighboring "countries" (e.g., the discharge of polluted waste water into the Rhine, or air pollution which causes forest damage).

(2) Countries (or their microeconomic units) "export" their pollution to unclaimed areas. The assessment and valuation of welfare costs depends on the level of individual and collective social consciousness. Since there is no welfare function for the "Global Society", the question is neither actual nor expected, as damages are not commensurable and a consensus for their elimination or prevention on the international level cannot be reached.

4. Ecological aspects of international trade in goods and services

There are some aspects which should be taken into account, mainly the following four:

(1) The slogan "Pollution is being exported" (Wirtschaftswoche, 1976, p. 56), can be proved by various means. Turned around, it can also be interpreted to mean that exports are promoted at the cost of the domestic environment. The economic and export structures of individual countries determine the "pollution intensity" that the exporting country must accept (*Glaser/Walter* 1976, p. 60). Taking this relationship into account (assuming that the same ecological standards were to apply in every country) "German exports created an overall higher environmental cost than did those of the USA" (whose exports are predominantly in the service and agricultural sectors).

(2) Economic policy decisions made in order to eliminate or restrict pollution have also stimulated an international trade with new investment equipment: Environmental technology, with its relevant capital goods, claims a solid and growing role in international economic relations. The USA, for example, realized aproximately 11 billion US-$ in export earnings per year in the late 1970s in this manner.

(3) Environmental requirements have, however, also contributed to the fact that the elimination of the relevant waste products became an internationally salable good; the OECD estimates that in the late

1970s, its export volume between member states reached approximately 2 billion US-$. Additionally, recycled products can become a significant part of international trade.

(4) Recently, discussion took place regarding the volume of chemical product exports to developing countries (e.g., herbicides, pesticides, etc.) which have long since been prohibited in the industrial countries (*Neumaier* 1982, p. 15). Furthermore, the question was posed, to what extent exports coming from developing countries are connected with considerable ecological damage (e.g., the import of tropical wood, which results in the clearing of tropical rainforests and causes irreversible erosion).

These *normative* judgements are closely related to arguments that the environmental damages, which especially manifest themselves in international economic relations, are a result of the affluence of the industrial countries and of the underdevelopment in the Third World.

5. World-wide industrialization and ecological impact

The "Group of 77" (Peru, 1975) has declared that by the year 2000, the developing countries should have a 25 % share of the global industrial output (which is currently at 10 %). It is not doubted that such an industrialization process will have a tremendous impact on the ecological environment: The first stage of processing raw materials to semi-manufactured products causes quite a bit of non-market and social costs. West German experience has shown that in the iron- and steel-industry, as well as in chemical production units, double the share of total investment is needed (10 %) in comparison to the situation of manufacturing industries in general (4.7 %) for environmental protection: Nine tenths of this volume is used for protection of water and air. Because capital is scare in developing countries, it is impossible for them to accumulate enough in this respect. Furthermore, the internalization of negative external technological effects (non-market relations have to be changed into market relations on the microeconomic level) will decrease the international competitiveness and shift the internal income distribution. In the mid of the 1970s, the USA imposed environmental controls, which increased total production costs by an average of 1.71 %. A breakdown thereof shows the following increases: Paper and pulp production 2.85 %, chemistry 4.0 %, petro chemistry (refinery) 4.78 %, and paint production 5.1 %. These figures show that international coordination of environmental measures is needed to avoid a distortion in the competetiveness regarding international trade. On the other hand, supplementary capital aid should be conceptualized in favor of developing countries in the field of environmental protection.

6. International trade in agricultural products

The demand for agriculture and forestry in industrialized countries can have a substantial negative impact on the environment of developing countries. The main reason is that developing countries have not yet established a framework or legislation to avoid a negative ecological impact. Findings of some case studies demonstrating this interdependence between international trade and ecological damage are available:

a) The heavily increased export of high quality wood has destroyed great parts of tropical forests, thereby irreversibly eliminating flora and fauna. The publication "Global 2000" (1980) has described the negative relation between wood exports and the devastation of forests. But this problem can only be solved through *national* regulation undertaken by the export countries themselves and not by discrimination in international trade. This decision process could be supported by increasing official development aid (ODA) in order to generate employment opportunities in Third World countries.

b) Food aid distributed by western governments and their donor agencies has been known to have a negative impact on the ecological situation in the recipient country. Case studies describe the starting point of the market distortion through food aid, followed by an exhaustion of arable land by, for example, overgrazing of pastures, which ends in a "desertification by institutionalized food aid" (*Wijkmann/Timberlake* 1986; *Zimen* 1985).

There is a common opinion that high population growth rates are the main reason for ecological destruction in less developed countries. Nevertheless, industrialized countries should realize that international relations play an important role in avoidance or reduction of environmental and ecological damage. Therefore, a new dimension of international cooperation needs to be reconsidered in this field.

7. International movements of capital with respect to ecological aspects

Two issues were discussed under this heading:

(1) Foreign private direct investment in developing countries in which there are lower environmental obligations.

(2) Official development aid (ODA) is transferred into the implementation of projects, which are potentially dangerous to the environment. Recently, a thesis stating that individual developing countries, under forced industrialization, due to very high debt services, have had to accept environmental damage as a necessary evil: An analysis of causal factors could, however, not thoroughly analyze the problem presented by this kind of interrelationship!

As far as foreign private direct investment is concerned, some case studies (IFO, Munich) illustrate the reasons why entrepreneurs have decided to start production in developing countries. The main arguments for investing abroad are the following[1]:

74 % (1974/1978) and 70 % (1978/1981) - to secure markets for their products; 40 % to avoid import barriers; 58 % and 64 % to save wage costs - and merely 1.5 % and 3.6 % respectively, to increase profits by using lower environmental standards! Other empirical studies have indicated that 10 % of foreign enterprises were established in order to avoid additional production costs in their home country (G. *Knödgen*). Nevertheless, foreign investors are aware that differing cost levels for ecological conditions exist, which have to be paid for by the enterprises.

Another consideration is quite important: One third of German entrepreneurs expect that in those foreign countries being considered, the costs of ecological measures will increase within the next five years. Regardless, they do not intend to retain foreign investments due to this reason. Even in subsidiaries abroad, they invest in the same environmentally oriented technical equipment, which is used "at home". They believe that the additional investment in the future would cost more than investment in "a package approach", which today covers the ecological requirements of tomorrow (a cost saving

---

[1] The answers are weighted by the number of employees. More than one answer is possible. Therefore, the total exceeds 100.

argument in the long run). In the near future, developing countries will implement stronger measures than they have in the past, therefore, favoring the "integrated investment approach", which already considers environmental problems.

Taking into account that more than 10 billion US-$ (1985) have been realized annually in foreign private direct investment in Third World countries, there is a growing responsibility for foreign investors to find the "right solution" in developing countries!

8. Ecological impact of development projects

In 1986, members of the OECD transferred 15.2 billion US-$ (net) of official development aid (ODA) and offered additional loans of 21.2 billion US-$. Those investments financed from abroad have an economic *and* ecological impact, mainly in agricultural and rural projects. In the last few years, new planning techniques have been developed to avoid or to minimize negative external effects. No doubt, there is a conflict between the economic and the ecological objectives. Consequently, development policy should try to combine both. The objectives of official development aid incorporate the environmental norms. Regarding this problem, the official German development policy can make the following contributions: (a) The conceptualization of economic projects needs to be complemented by ecological (ex-ante) measures: This approach is more closely related to financial means. (b) Special environmental projects should be financed to protect natural resources and to eliminate ecological damage (ex-post measures).

Last but not least, an ecologically minded policy is required in developing countries themselves. A new dimension of ecological consultation needs to be introduced into the "political dialogue". International transfers of technology and extended services should be offered within the same context.

9. Public goods within the frame of international economic relations

Presently, the concept of public goods coming from beyond national borders is being reconsidered. With the increasing geographical mobility of ecological damage (high sea, ocean floor, atmosphere, Antarctic, etc.), the ability to organize interests to eliminate or avoid the damage decreases: The "legal claims for property rights need to be implemented to a broader extent" (*Wolfrum* 1984). These "supra-country goals" can "stand in contradiction to the state sovereignty and territorial integrity" (*Dicke* 1986, p. 111). An over-intensified use of the public goods ("environment") in the international sphere (e.g., outside of the national territories) can be observed. The problem of this "free-rider behavior" has been recognized, but adequate solutions are not feasible.

10. Resource exhaustion from an international viewpoint

This issue has been expressed as follows: "The market allocation of exhaustible resources causes intertemporal external effects". In other words: To what extent do we currently use (through international trade) non-renewable raw materials, the lack of which will endanger the standard of living or existence of future generations?

Once again, the limits of normative approaches and judgements become obvious, namely in intertemporal welfare comparisons, the estimations of future technical progress, and the uncertainty of raw material reserves.

11. Concluding remarks

On the national level, there are great difficulties in coordinating economic and ecological objectives. Even greater problems arise in cases where neighboring countries look for environmental solutions to externalities along their borders. Last but not least, the greatest difficulties exist on the international level, where they seem not to be solvable at this time. There are quite a lot of reasons for diverging opinions: (1) the normative approaches to handling this challenge for economic research, (2) the complexity of the problem itself, (3) the difficulty in distinguishing between market and non-market relations, and (4) the problem of measuring the damages, currently as well as in the long run.

This paper has tried mainly to illustrate the interdependence between "economy" and "ecology", which necessitated a systematic classification of external diseconomies and social costs. Further, specific problems have been enumerated, which should be considered in future research. The answers still have to be found, and an interdisciplinary approach could be taken into account to do so.

In the last years, the perception of world problems as economic and ecological conflicts has led to the construction of global models. It is impossible, however, to say just what they have taught us about the world. The well known *Forester/Meadows* model, "The Limits to Growth" (1972), has lead to critical remarks, which were later used in the model of the *Bariloche* Group (1976) in "Catastrophy or New Society". The World Bank has also covered the specific topic in: "How Vulnerable Are Developing Countries to External Shocks?", which has been available since 1974. An "OECD-Model" focuses on the developed countries related to this question: The "Interlink-Model" (OECD) analyzes international trade and financial linkages. The IASSA has presented a model which discusses the basis for international food production and distribution solutions and finally, the MOIRA-Model analyzes international agricultural relations.

In almost all of these models, ecological problems are implicitly covered. The most interesting approach was presented by the Research Group "GLOBUS-MODEL", which includes, more than others, the decison-making structure of governments.

Some of these models related to international economic relationships can be used to evaluate the conflicts between "Economy and Ecology".

References

Ahn, S.-K., Ausländische Privatinvestitionen in Südkorea - Voraussetzungen und Auswirkungen auf die sozialökonomische Entwicklung. Eine Fallstudie, Mainz/München 1980

Bariloche-Report, Catastrophy or New Society, Washington D.C. 1981

Council on Environmental Quality, The Global 2000 Report to the President, US-State Department, Washington D.C. 1980

Dams, Th., Entwicklungsländer: Auslandsinvestitionen und Technologietransfer, in: Zielsetzung Partnerschaft: Edition Dräger-Stiftung, Stuttgart 1985

Dams, Th. (ed.), Auswirkungen ausländischer Privatinvestitionen in Entwicklungsländern, KAEF-Materialien, Bonn 1980

Dicke, K., Grenzüberschreitende Umweltverschmutzung als völkerrechtliches Problem. in: M. *Haendcke-Hoppe*/K. *Merkel* (eds.), Umweltschutz in beiden Teilen Deutschlands, Berlin 1986

Dunning, J.H., Explaining the International Direct Investment Position of Countries: Towards a Dynamic or Developmental Approach, in: Weltwirtschaftliches Archiv, Vol. 117, Kiel 1981

Endres, A., Umwelt- und Ressourcenökonomie, Darmstadt 1985

Fritsch, B., Zur Theorie und Systematik der volkswirtschaftlichen Kosten, in: G. *Gäfgen* (ed.), Grundlagen der Wirtschaftspolitik, Köln 1970

Fröbel, F./*Heinrichs*, J./*Kreye*, O., Umbruch in der Weltwirtschaft, Hamburg 1986

Glaeser, B./*Walter*, I., Internationale Wirtschaft: Verschmutzung wird exportiert, in: Wirtschaftswoche, Düsseldorf, No. 41/1976

Haberler, G. von, Der internationale Handel, Berlin 1933

Haberler, G. von, The Theory of International Trade with its Applications to Commercial Policy, London, Edinburgh, Glasgow 1986

Hoffmann, L., Technologietransfer in Entwicklungsländern -Analytische Konzepte und wirtschaftspolitische Aspekte, in: Zielsetzung Partnerschaft. Edition Dräger-Stiftung, Stuttgart 1985

Holtham, G./*Llewellyn*, J./*Richardson*, P./*Samuelson*, L., Representing Recent Policy Concerns, in: INTERLINK - A Progress Report, in: H. *Giersch* (ed.), Probleme und Perspektiven der weltwirtschaftlichen Entwicklung, Berlin 1985, pp. 505 -518

IIASA, The Perception of World Problems, in: Perceptions and Analyses of World Problems (chapter 1), Paris 1986

Jahrreiß, W., Zur Theorie der Direktinvestitionen im Ausland, Berlin 1984

Jöhr, W.A., Das Bariloche-Modell. Ein lateinamerikanisches Weltmodell, in: Schweizerische Zeitschrift für Volkswirtschaft und Statistik, no. 2, 1981, pp. 113 - 172

Kapp, W., Sozialkosten, in: Handwörterbuch der Sozialwissenschaften, Stuttgart 1956.

Knirsch, J., Pestizide Ex- und Import, in: Buko - Materialien, Hamburg, (no date)

Knödgen, G./*Sprenger*, R.-U., Umweltschutz und internationaler Wettbewerb, in: Ifo-Schnelldienst, 1 - 2, München 1981

Kojima, K., Japanese Direct Foreign Investment, Tokyo 1978

Larsen, F./*Llewellyn*, J./*Potto*, S., International Economic Linkages, in: OECD Economic Studies, No. 1/1983, pp. 65 - 91

Liem, N.-H., Ausländische Privatinvestitionen auf den Philippinen - Voraussetzungen und Auswirkungen auf die sozialökonomische Entwicklung. Eine Fallstudie, Mainz/München 1980

Meadows, D. et al., The Limits of Growth, Stuttgart 1972

Meadows, D./*Richardson*, J./*Bruckmann*, G., Groping in the Dark, Bristol 1982, pp.7- 17

Neumaier, T., Weniger Agrarchemie in die Dritte Welt? in: Entwicklung und Zusammenarbeit, Bonn 2/1982

OECD/DAC, Twenty-Five Years of Development Co-Operation - A Review, Paris 1985

Oppenländer, K.H, Auslandsinvestitionen und außenwirtschaftlicher Technologietransfer, in: Zielsetzung Partnerschaft. Edition Dräger-Stiftung, Stuttgart 1985

Pigou, A.C., The Welfare of Economics, London 1920

Pollak, C./*Riedel*, J., Motive und Ziele der industriellen Zusammenarbeit mit Schwellenländern, München 1984

Pollak, C./*Riedel*, J., Das Engagement deutscher Unternehmen in Entwicklungsländern - Stand und Perspektiven, in: Ifo-Schnelldienst, München, 21/1984

Ruppert, W., Produktionsstandorte der Industrie im Urteil der Unternehmen, in: Ifo-Schnelldienst, München, 19/1979

Samuelson, P.A., Welfare Economics and International Trade, in: American Economic Review, Vol. 28, 1938

Schlieper, U., Externe Effekte, in: HdWW, Stuttgart 1980

Siebert, H., Ökonomische Theorie der Umwelt, Tübingen 1978

Vernon, R., International Investment and International Trade in the Product Cycle, in: Quarterly Journal of Economics, 80th vol., 1966

Vieser, D., Ausländische Privatinvestitionen im Senegal. Eine Fallstudie über Struktur, Rahmenbedingungen und Auswirkungen in einem AKP-Land, Berlin 1982

Waelbroeck, J., How Vulnerable are Developing Countries to External Shocks? An Application of the World Bank's Sensitivity Analyses Model, in: H. *Giersch* (ed.), Probleme und Perspektiven der weltwirtschaftlichen Entwicklung, Berlin 1985, pp. 487- 504.

Wijkmann, A./*Timberlake*, L., Die Rache der Schöpfung, München 1986

Wissenschaftszentrum Berlin (WZB) - Modeling: An Overview, in: Perceptions and Analyses of World Problems, chapter 6, Paris 1986

Wolfrum, R., Die Internationalisierung staatsfreier Räume. Die Entwicklung einer internationalen Verwaltung für Antarktis, Weltraum, Hohe See und Meeresboden, Berlin 1984

Zimen, E., Rettet die Dritte Welt vor unserem Aktionismus, in: Natur, No. 3, München 1985

Rate of Protection and Returns to Farm Work: Dynamic Aspects of Price Support Policies

Yuko Arayama

1. Introduction

All developed countries, without exception, have been protecting their agriculture. The main purpose for this protectionism was twofold at the beginning: increasing agricultural production and "improving" the income level of farm households. Since many countries are now suffering from overprotection of agricultural products, the only reason left for them to keep a high protection rate should be "improving" returns to farm work, which are low compared with the market wages. Returns to farm work can be improved by raising commodity prices. Yet this argument holds true only in a static framework. Dynamic theory cannot support it.

The purpose of this paper is to emphasize the importance of dynamic aspects of price support policies. Effects of any policy can accumulate over time, and can result in many types of economic distortions. Regardless of this apparent logic, too little attention has been paid to dynamic aspects of price support policies.

The rest of this paper will be organized as follows: in the next section, we will review two theoretical models on price support policies. Section 3 compares costs of production in Japan with those in West Germany and the U.S. Section 4 investigates the effects of a high rate of agricultural protection on returns to farm work. The last section will consider recent arguments for liberalization of agricultural commodities in terms of the dynamic aspects reviewed in this paper.

2. Theoretical framework

We can analyse the effects of price support policies on the rate of returns to farm work and farm land through the theory of derived demand. Derived demand is defined as demand for factors of production derived from the demand for final goods. The details of derived demand have been studied by *Marshall* (1961) and *Hicks* (1963). *Floyd* (1965) applied this theory of derived demand to an analysis of price support policies. His theoretical model had a static, partial equilibrium framework, and his model did not have any implications for a dynamic aspect of price support policies. However, we can use his model to infer the dynamics of price support policies, since the model shows the effects of price support policies on the rates of returns to factors of production in terms of elasticities. If we interpret them as long-run elasticities, his model can analyse long-run implications of price support policies. If we interpret them as short-run elasticities, it can give short-run implications of price support policies.

Now we introduce a basic structure of the *Floyd* model. The model consists of the following six equations: 1) homogeneous agricultural production function which utilizes farm land and labor for its inputs, 2) two first order conditions for maximization of farm output, 3) farm land supply function, 4) labor supply function for farm production, 5) demand function for farm products[1].

$$X = f(a,b) \tag{1}$$

$$P_a = f_a P_x \tag{2}$$

$$P_b = f_b P_x \tag{3}$$

$$a = P_a^{\beta_a} \tag{4}$$

$$b = P_b^{\beta_b} \tag{5}$$

$$X = P_x^{\eta} \tag{6}$$

---

[1] f_a and f_b indicate the marginal product of land and labor respectively.

In these equations, a indicates farm land, b indicates labor, X is farm product. P_a, P_b and P_x are price of farm land, wages and price of farm products respectively. $ß_a$, $ß_b$ and η show elasticity of land supply, elasticity of labor supply, and elasticity of demand for farm products.

By combining and differentiating (2) and (4), and (3) and (5) respectively, we get the following results:

(7) $$E_a = \frac{\sigma+ß_b}{\sigma+s_aß_b+s_bß_a}$$

(8) $$E_b = \frac{\sigma+ß_a}{\sigma+s_aß_b+s_bß_a}$$

(9) $$e_a = \frac{(\sigma+ß_b)\,ß_a}{\sigma+s_aß_b+s_bß_a}$$

(10) $$e_b = \frac{(\sigma+ß_a)\,ß_b}{\sigma+s_aß_b+s_bß_a}$$

E_a and E_b are elasticities of product prices on the returns to land and labor respectively. e_a and e_b indicate elasticities of product prices on the amount of factors of production. σ indicates an elasticity substitution between farm land and farm labor. Furthermore, S_a and S_b are shares of the respective factor of production in the price of output.

These four elasticities are indicating the effects of farm price support on the returns to factors of production and on the amount of factors used in farm production. Namely, the effect of price support on the returns to a factor is larger when its elasticity of supply is smaller, and the effect is smaller when its elasticity of supply is larger. Concerning the amount of factors used in production, farm price support policies will result in large increases in a factor of production (used in production), when the elasticity of supply of the factor of production is large, and vice versa.

Before applying this model to an analysis of price support policies, it is necessary to evaluate the value of parameters. Firstly, elasticity of substitution between farm land and farm labor (σ) will not have a large value in the short-run, but might reach a value around unity in the long-run.

Secondly, we will consider that elasticity of supply of farm labor exceeds that of farm land. The elasticity could be larger through reallocation of work hours between farm work and off-farm work in countries like Japan, where the share of farm household members engaged in off-farm work is very high. In countries which have high labor mobility like the U.S., the elasticity of supply of farm labor should be high. On the other hand, elasticity of supply of farm labor is low in West Germany and Japan since supply of land itself is very limited. Even in a land-abundant country like the U.S., many studies indicate low elasticity of supply of farm land.

On these premises price support policies (raising output prices) tend to increase returns to farm land without raising returns to farm labor due to the low elasticity of land supply compared with that of labor supply. Price support at the same time promotes work hours in farm production through an increase in farm employment or through reallocation of time. In other words, price support policies will fail to increase returns to farm labor, contrary to their "expected" effects.

According to this model, farm employment in Japan should have been increasing due to price support policies. On the contrary, farm employment in Japan has been decreasing over time. We can observe similar situations in West Germany and the U.S. How can we explain these contradictions?

As income increases, farm employment decreases due to low income elasticity of demand for farm products. Generally, income elasticity of demand for farm products is less than unity. Therefore, as an economy grows, the share of farm products decreases, and that of non-farm products increases. Accordingly, the share of the labor force engaged in farm work declines. Therefore, employment structures are also strongly affected by demand conditions.

How can we analyse the effect of price support policies of growing countries? *Johnson* (1973) analysed this situation as follows:

"... in the long-run an increase in output price will have little effect on the value of labor or its wage rate. The primary effect would be upon the quantity of labor engaged in agriculture. Note that this conclusion does not say that five or any other number of years after the output price has been increased and maintained the wage rates would not be any higher than at the beginning of the period. What is said is that at some not distant date in the future the wage rate in agriculture would be approximately the same where or not the output price had been increased. In an economy with rising real per capita incomes the return to farm labour would increase, as it has historically".

Figure 1 shows the dynamic effect of price support policies on the rate of return to farm work and farm employment. The vertical axis indicates time-series of the rate of return to farm work and the rate of decrease in farm employment. The rate of return to farm work should increase as the market wage rate increases through labor migration from the agricultural sector to the non-agricultural sector in order to keep equilibrium returns. Since wages have been rising several percentage points every year in non-agricultural sectors, employment in the farm sector should have been declining at a certain rate every year. Specifically, employment in the agricultural sector decreases and the returns to farm work increase at a certain rate, if no price support policy is adopted to improve the returns to farm work. Labor migration from the agricultural sector to non-agricultural sectors is induced by possible wage differentials between them.

Now we will analyse effects of once and for all price increases on the returns to farm work and farm employment. Special attention will be placed upon the distinction between short-run and long-run effects and the transition.

Short-run effects of once and for all price increases of a farm product at time t_1 are as follows. As the *Floyd* model showed, an increase in price of a farm product will result in higher returns to farm work. This increase in returns to farm work depends on supply elasticities of farm labor and farm land and their elasticity of substitution in production. The wage differential between agricultural and non-agricultural sectors will decline due to an increase in returns to farm work. The rate of decrease in farm labor will drop due to this reduction of the wage differential.

Figure 1: Returns to Farm Work and Employment in Agricultural Sector

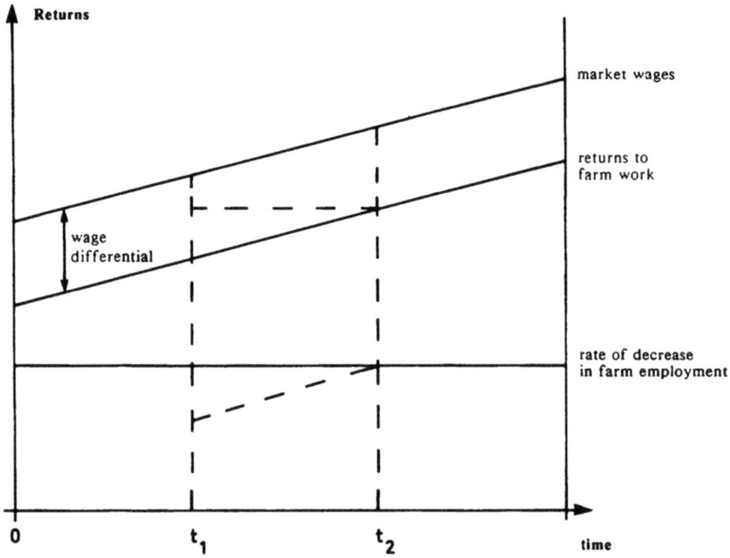

Table 1: Costs of Wheat Production, 1979-1984 (in ¥ / 60 kg; in brackets: percentages)

	West Germany		Japan	
seed	183	(7.8)	577	(5.7)
fertilizer	491	(26.6)	1179	(11.7)
insecticide	190	(10.3)	258	(2.6)
gasoline	131	(7.1)	231	(2.3)
rental fee	237	(12.8)	1309	(13.0)
buildings & land improvement	18	(1.0)	161	(1.6)
machines	74	(4.0)	1900	(18.8)
labor	127	(6.9)	2336	(23.1)
interest	69	(3.7)	394	(3.9)
land	368	(19.9)	1955	(19.3)
TOTAL	1850	(100.0)	10100	(100.0)

Note: 1 DM = ¥ 107.5

Source: Analytical Report on EC Farm Management (1986).

The period between t_1 and t_2 in the figure indicates the transition. As long as the rate of reduction of farm labor declines, the rate of increase in returns to farm work also declines. The wage differential starts increasing again due to this decline in the rate of increase in returns to farm work. As a result of the wage differential, labor migration from the agricultural sector to non-agricultural sectors increases again. After a certain time, the rate of decrease in farm labor returns to the original level and the returns to farm work turn back to the original time path.

This model shows that an increase in output price has no long term effect on the returns to farm work and the rate of decrease in farm labor. If this is the case, what has the one time price support policy brought about? The answer for this question is a delay in reallocation of productive resources. Higher returns to farm work retain farm labor from migration to non-agricultural sectors.

This model implies that output prices must keep rising in order to sustain higher returns to farm work, because a one time increase in output prices can raise the returns to farm work for an only limited period, and have no long term effect on them. This is important when we analyse long term effects of price support policies. Since the effect of this delay in labor adjustment can accumulate, using price support policies to improve the returns to farm work should result in excessive labor in the agricultural sector. This distortion in factor allocation should have caused serious inefficiencies in production for the countries which have been using price support measures for a long period of time.

3. Cost of production

This section will make an international cost comparison of wheat and rice production[2]. Firstly, we compare costs of wheat production between West Germany and Japan based on the *Analytical Report on EC Farm Management*. Table 1 shows 5 year-averages (1979-84) of costs of wheat production in West Germany and Japan. Costs of production per 60 kg in Japan is 10,100 yen and about six times more expensive than than in West Germany where costs of production are

[2] There are some difficulties for these comparisons. The main reasons for this are: 1) differences in the type of management or in the composition of farm products, 2) different ways of taking statistics, or different notations in statistics among countries, 3) unstable exchange rates, and so on.

1,850 yen. Especially labor costs and machinery costs are much higher in Japan in terms of both value and share in total costs. For example, Japanese labor costs (2,336 yen) have reached about twenty times the level of German labor costs (127 yen). Machinery costs have also reached seventeen times the amount of costs in Germany. On the other hand, the share of fertilizer, insecticide, and gasoline in total production costs in West Germany is higher than in Japan. But these costs in West Germany are still lower than in Japan in terms of value. As far as land costs are concerned, West Germany and Japan are keeping similar shares.

Secondly, 1984 costs of rice production for the U.S. and Japan are compared. Table 2 indicates that total cost of rice production per 60 kg is 15,600 yen in Japan, and 2,575 yen in the U.S. Japanese total cost was about six times larger than in the U.S. Labor cost and land cost are much higher in Japan compared with the U.S. Labor cost is 3,904 yen in Japan and 203 yen in the U.S. Similarly, land cost is 3,953 yen in Japan and 353 yen in the U.S.

The two comparisons made above can be summarized as follows: 1) total costs of both wheat and rice production are extremely (about six times as) high in Japan compared with West Germany and the U.S. 2) In terms of cost shares, labor cost is a major component in Japan; in contrast, purchasing inputs (such as fertilizer, insecticide and gasoline) take a major share in West Germany and U.S.

4. Protection and rate of return to farm work

Tables 1 and 2 tell us that Japan has been keeping a high protection rate in wheat and rice production compared with West Germany and U.S. over a long period. As a result of these high rates of protection, costs of wheat production in Japan have reached as much as six times those in West Germany, and costs of rice production in Japan has also become six times higher than in the U.S.

Could the high rate of agricultural protection have successfully raised the rate of return to farm work? This section will investigate the effectiveness and consequences of agricultural protection. Figure 2 has plotted the time-series of hourly returns to 1) white collar type work, 2) blue collar type work, 3) day's work, and 4) farm work for male farm household members during the period between 1964 and 1984. These series of data on returns to work are computed by

Table 2: Costs of Rice Production, 1984 (in ¥ / 60 kg; in brackets: percentages)

	U. S.		Japan	
seed, fertilizer, insecticide, gasoline, rental fee, buildings & land inprovement	1600	(62)	7144	(46)
machines	481	(18)	3845	(25)
labor	203	(8)	3904	(25)
interest	145	(6)	638	(4)
land	358	(14)	3953	(25)
TOTAL	2575	(100)	15609	(100)

Note: $ 1 = ¥ 169.6

Source: *Hattori* (1987)

Table 3: Summary Statistics, 1984

(unit: 10,000)

	West Germany	Japan	U. S.
Population	6,118	12,002	23,660
Working Persons in Agriculture	93	534	195
Share in Work Force	3.1 %	8.6 %	1.8 %
Number of Farm Households	74	452	240
Land per Farm Household	16.2 ha	1.2 ha	179.7 ha
Share of Agr. Production in GNP	2.0 %	3.3 %	2.0 %

Source: Analytical Report on EC Farm Management (1986).

Figure 2: Returns to Farm Work and Market Wages

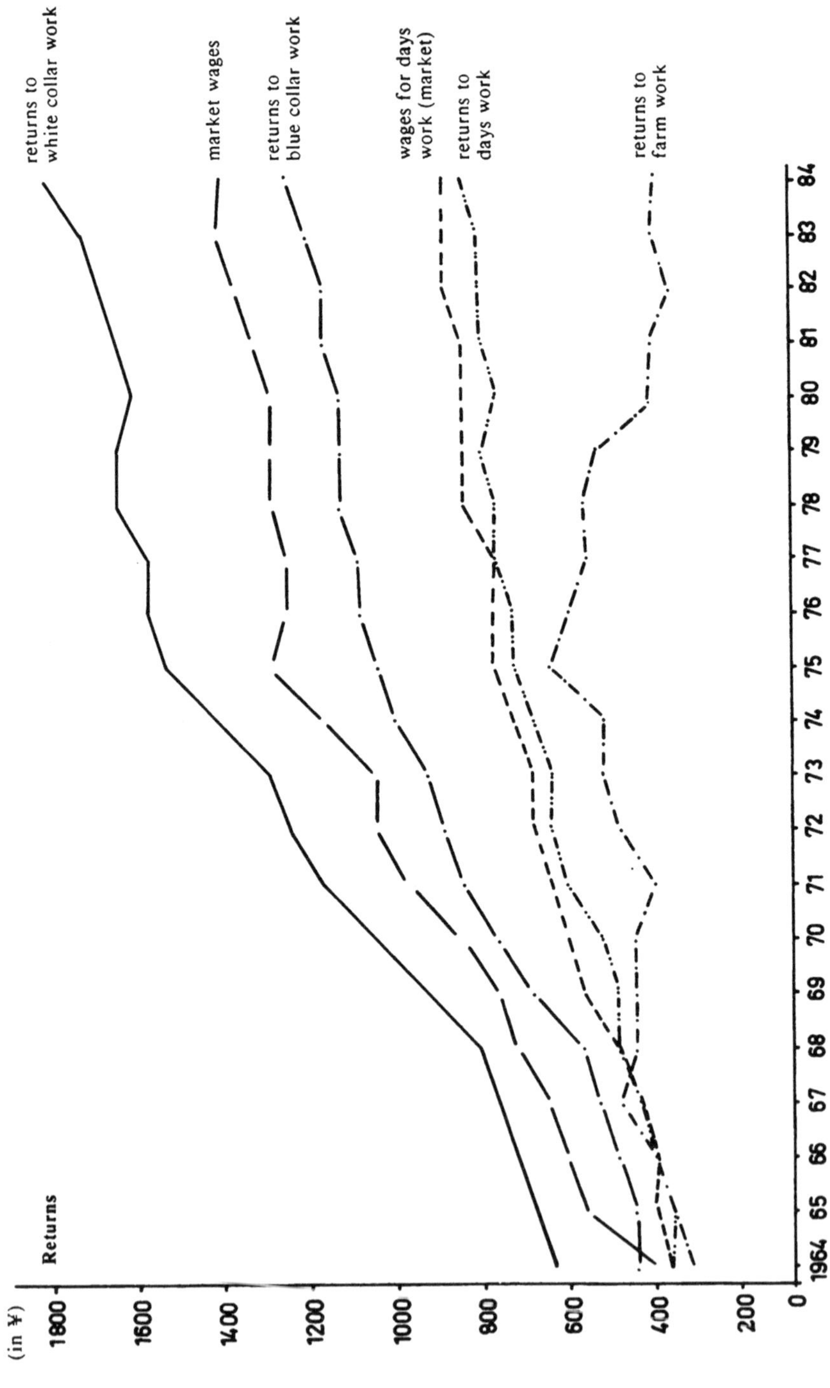

utilizing the Survey Report on Farm Household Economy[3]. Additionally, market wages based on data from *Wages Census* are plotted in the same figure. We can see that the high rate of agricultural protection has hardly succeeded to raise the returns to farm work. On the contrary, returns to farm work have started to decline since 1975.

Why have exorbitantly high labor costs in Japan, which are as much as twenty times higher than in West Germany and the U.S., failed to raise returns to farm work? The possible explanation was given in the section on the theoretical framework. When labor is supplied elastically, raising the price of farm products will not improve the returns to farm work, instead, it retains the work force within the agricultural sector, which otherwise should migrate to other sectors. For this reason, agricultural production has become less efficient.

Table 3 shows a comparison of the major agricultural statistics of West Germany, Japan, and U.S., and provides evidence which could support the dynamic aspects of price support policies. Comparing the agriculture of these three countries based on the dynamic considerations reveals that the share of a working person in agriculture is highest in Japan, which also has been keeping the highest rate of agricultural protection. Namely, 8.6 % of the work force is engaged in agriculture in Japan, but this share is only 3.1 % in West Germany and only 1.8 % in the U.S. The number of farm households, 4.5 million, is also highest in Japan. On the other hand, farm size has remained smallest in Japan; this is possibly due to high land prices resulting from high price support policies.

5. Protectionism or liberalization

In the recent arguments on world trade of agricultural commodities, domestic high prices of agricultural commodities are attributed to the results of protectionism. This might be true. Then, what kind of economic mechanisms are relevant in this process? What are the consequences of protectionism?

This study has shown that the returns to farm work have not successfully been increased regardless of high prices of agricultural

---

[3] Data from *Wage Census* is also utilized in order to derive these time-series.

commodities, contrary to the economic implication of the static theory of protection. It has turned out that this "puzzle" could be explained by taking dynamic aspects of price support policy into consideration. This paper also emphasized the importance of long-term consequences of price support policies. It must be recognized that maintaining farm price support policies for a long period of time should have resulted in accumulated distortions in factor markets. Namely, factors of production, such as labor, capital, and land, are mis-allocated in many developed countries.

This world should be full of economic distortions. To make matters worse, these distortions have been accumulated over a long range of time. Under these circumstances, immediate liberalization could be a fallible remedy, since adjustment in many factor markets takes time. Our economic intuitions should deny "liberalization" which results in sudden changes in a part of the factor markets. In the existence of any "fixed" distortion, second best policy is an optimal policy.

What kind of policy must be taken for liberalization as a second best? We have not yet reached a concrete answer for this question. But, we believe that the evidence shown in this study should have convinced the reader of the importance of dynamic aspects of price support policies.

References

Center For Agricultural Development and Training, Analytical Report on EC Farm Management, 1986

Floyd, J., The Effects of Farm Price Supports on the Returns to Land and Labor in Agriculture, Journal of Political Economy, 72, April 1965

Hattori, S., Amerika no Kome to Gyuuniku (Rice and Beef Production in USA), Osaka (Fuminkyoukai) 1987

Hicks, J., The Theory of Wages, 2nd edition, London (Macmillan) 1963

Johnson, D. G., World Agriculture in Disarray, New York (St. Martin's Press) 1973

Lipsey, R. G./*Lancaster*, K. J., The General Theory of Second Best, Review of Economic Studies, 24, 1956/57, pp. 11-32

Marshall, A., Principles of Economics, 9th edition, London (Macmillan) 1961

Financial Assistance Available for Setting up Business in the Federal Republic of Germany

Wolfgang Hilke

1. Introduction

The German "Mittelstand", which means the small and medium sized businesses, represents the driving force in the West German economy and in economic development. Out of about 1.9 million West German business firms, about 90 % or 1.7 million (*not* including agriculture and forestry) can be classified as small to medium sized businesses.

These 1.7 million businesses are made up as follows (cf. Wirtschaftsmacht Mittelstand ..., 1986, p. 8):

- 381,000 production enterprises (including craft trades) with an annual turnover of over DM 100,000,
- 287,000 commercial enterprises with an annual turnover of over DM 250,000,
- 379,000 service enterprises with an annual turnover of over DM 100,000,
- 630,000 very small businesses with a turnover below the above figures.

Even when disregarding the 630,000 very small businesses, the remaining 1.05 million small and medium sized businesses employ as many as 10.8 million people, in other words, about 55 % of the 19.6 million West Germans in paid employment (not counting the civil service). Of the total turnover within the private sector of the economy, about 48 % can be attributed to the 1.05 million small and medium sized businesses.

As can be clearly seen from these figures, small and medium sized companies have enormous significance for the German economy. Consequently, it becomes obvious why the central government and the regional governments of the Federation are keenly interested in maintaining and supporting the small and medium sized companies and in providing financial aids for starting up new businesses.

Promotion and support takes many forms. One of the most significant is "direct financial assistance". This start-up assistance is urgently needed, because most people interested in starting up their own business neither have sufficient capital of their own, nor adequate security for credits necessary to set up in business.

The objective of this paper is to give a general idea of the most important financial aids provided by the federal government and by the government of the State of Baden-Württemberg in setting up businesses.

In addition to the commercial bank of the person intending to set up in business, the following credit institutes are involved in providing financial assistance:
- DAB Deutsche Ausgleichsbank (German Compensatory Bank, formerly the "Lastenausgleichsbank", German Equalization Bank) of Bonn-Bad Godesberg;
- LKB Landeskreditbank (Regional State Credit Bank) of Karlsruhe, State of Baden-Württemberg
- Bürgschaftsbank (Surety Bank) Baden-Württemberg, Stuttgart.

2. General terms and conditions for granting financial aid

First, there are several provisions which have to be observed when applying for financial assistance.

Project worthiness:
When new businesses are set up in the Federal Republic or in Baden-Württemberg, only those projects are considered for support which:
- are worthy of support in economic and business administrative terms (reasonableness),
- increase economic performance and competitiveness and
- promise a long-term economic success (full existence of the self-employed individual).

Investment finance only:
As a rule, credits are given for financing *investments* with long-term credit requirements only, i.e. for financing the following:

- property, premises as well as the necessary machinery and facilities;
- the purchasing price of an existing enterprise;
- the purchase of an active interest (e.g. interest as partner or limited partner with managerial authority).

Exception: the LKB also provides pro rata support of "working funds requirements", e.g. the money needed for establishing the first goods in stock.

Proportional finance (i.e. subsidiary principle):
The money is intended only for proportional financing of projects; the applicant is expected to provide reasonable means of his own.

No follow-up finance:
The money may not be used for projects which have already been initiated at the time of application.

Specific purposes:
The loans are granted for specific purposes. Calling and use of the credit must be in portions. After completion of the project, evidence of use must be provided.

Addressees:
Trainees within commercial economy, especially in the following fields:
- manufacturing trade,
- commerce,
- craft trade,
- small businesses,
- catering and hotel trade,
- health professionals (physicians, dispensing chemists, others),
- the "economy related" professions, e.g. accountants, auditors, attorneys, advertising specialists, architects, chartered engineers in construction and surveying.

Personal requirements:
- minimum age 21 years, maximum age 50 years,
- evidence of professional and business qualifications (in craft trade: Master Craftsman's Certificate).

3. Credits available for setting up in business

3.1. Federal ERP fund ("Start-Up Program")

ERP stands for "European Recovery Program". Today's federal ERP fund for special purposes goes back to the *Marshall* Plan, which was in effect until 1957 and is today mainly used for providing incentives to the German economy (the statutory basis for funding is the ERP Economy Law, 1953). The following applies to ERP loans for promoting new business ventures (ERP Start-Up Program):

Projects supported (appropriation):
- setting up and purchasing businesses, as well as accompanying investments within 3 years after setting up business;
- take-over of active interests;
- procurement of first goods in stock or initial office equipment.

Entitlement:
Trainees within commercial economy (especially manufacturing trade, commerce and craft trade). Priority is given to applicants who, over a period of several years, have saved up their own capital with a credit institute.

Terms of the loan:
- interest rate: 8.5 % in 1990
- sum paid out: 100 %
- maximum amount: DM 300,000
- period: up to 10 years, for building projects up to 15 years, redemption-free for a maximum of 2 years.

Application procedure:
Applications may be submitted at any credit institute. The ERP loans are provided by the DAB, Bonn. Over the last years, more and more credit applications have been turned down. "In the ERP Start-Up Program, 2782 loan applications were refused in 1986. The refusal rate in that year is therefore 17.3 %. In the majority of cases the reasons were insufficient qualifications and doubts concerning the future viability of the business project" (DAB (ed.), Annual Report 1986, p. 47, translated by W.H.).

Table 1 shows how the loan granting volume of the ERP Start-Up Program by the DAB has developed between 1982 and 1988.

Table 1:
Development of the ERP Start-up Program

year	loan granting volume total	loan granting volume for Baden-Württemberg
1982	613.4 mio DM	132.7 mio DM = 21.6 %
1983	908.2 mio DM	175.5 mio DM = 19.3 %
1984	807.0 mio DM	148.8 mio DM = 18.4 %
1985	723.4 mio DM	149.0 mio DM = 20.6 %
1986	740.6 mio DM	160.4 mio DM = 21.7 %
1987	705.0 mio DM	152.0 mio DM = 21.6 %
1988	715.6 mio DM	156.8 mio DM = 21.9 %

Source: Deutsche Ausgleichsbank (ed.), Annual Reports 1982 ff.; Press release of the DAB from 6.1.1988, Mit Existenz-Investitionen von 3 Mrd DM bewirkt, p. 1

Table 2:
Development of the Loan Volume in the Supplementary Program I of the DAB

year	loan volume
1982	16.5 mio DM
1983	66.8 mio DM
1984	165.1 mio DM
1985	173.9 mio DM
1986	185.2 mio DM
1987	162.7 mio DM
1988	174.8 mio DM

Source: Deutsche Ausgleichsbank (ed.), Annual Reports 1982 ff.

3.2. Supplementary Program I of the Deutsche Ausgleichsbank (DAB)

This program was introduced in 1975 by the LAB (today: DAB). In case of more capital-intensive investments it is possible to extend this supplementary program by means of ERP credits, because both programs are not set off against each other when calculating the maximum loans permissible in each case (cf. DAB (ed.), Financial Assistance ..., p. 8).

Although the terms of the Supplementary Program I are slighty less favorable than those of the ERP funds, they still lie below the interest rates usually charged by banks. The DAB does not finance the interest reduction through official subsidies, but instead through its own proceeds (cf. DAB (ed.), Federal Credit Institute ..., p. 10). Corresponding to the profit situation, the volume of financial funding was increased from 16.5 million DM in 1982 to 175 million DM in 1988. "Thus, the start-up loans granted by the DAB represent a typical example of supplementing the official promotion measures, financed by central and regional governments, through supportive 'internal programs' by the central special credit institutes" (*Goldschmidt* 1985, p. 88, translated by W.H.). In detail, the following criteria apply (cf. DAB (ed.), Programs ..., p. 13 f.):

Projects supported/appropriation:
- investments for setting up in business for trainees in the field of commercial economy and in the economy-related professions; among them investments made during the initial stages of a business, provided they are connected with the foundation of the business;
- investments for securing the location (purchase of business premises used up to date, purchase of neighboring property, etc.) or for relocation of premises;
- investments in conjunction with establishing branches, under the condition that the present business does not provide an adequate basis of existence, as well as investments serving to expand product assortment or aiming to extend or change the range of services or products; increasing the goods in stock will also be considered in this context;
- investments for new and innovative products or processes;
- supplementary financing of the official promotion programs conducted by the DAB.

Entitlement:
Eligible are small and medium sized businesses within the commercial economy (requiring that they serve the co-operation of several, legally independent enterprises), as well as persons in economy-related professions.

Terms of the loan:
- loan amount: up to 50 % of costs eligible for support, no fixed upper limit;
- duration: up to 10 years, redemption-free for up to 2 years;
- interest rate: 8.25 % p.a. in 1990;
- sum paid out: 95 %;
- commitment fees: 0.25 % per month started, if the loan is not taken from the DAB by the last day of the month following the promise to grant a loan;
- securities: full risk for applicant's banker; if no securities are provided: DAB bond, commission: 0.5 % per annum on the allowance provided by the applicant's bank.

Application procedure:
Applications are to be submitted (on standard forms) to the local credit institute; the DAB reserves the right to make inquiries, requesting expert opinions from competent institutions.

Table 2 shows the development of the loan volume in the Supplementary Program I of the DAB.

3.3. Landeskreditbank (Regional State Credit Bank, LKB program 1)

In the State of Baden-Württemberg, the LKB Program 1 comprises the following provisions:

Projects supported/appropriation
(through loans for financing investments and working funds):
- start-ups in business, especially setting up or take-over of companies or offices of economically active professions, also active interests;
- consolidation of businesses for up to 5 years (in exceptions, for 7 years) following start-up.

Entitlement:
Trainees in trade, commerce and medium sized industries (provided the number of employees does not exceed 50), of the service sector, catering and hotel trade and of persons working as professionals not including health and legal professions).

Terms of the loan:
- amount: as a rule, up to one third of the costs eligible for assistance (= investment and working capital requirements); maximum DM 300,000, in exceptions DM 500,000 provided that no financial assistance was granted by the Federation (ERP);
- duration: up to 12 years (in case of building investments up to 20 years), redemption-free for up to 4 years;
- interest rate: 8 % p.a. (for entire term of loan);
- sum paid out: 98 %.

Application procedure:
via the applicant's bank to the LKB.

Some further information concerning the LKB Program 1: The loan granting procedure requires that the applicant furnishes evidence with regard to his professional and business qualifications and that he submits a promising business concept. Upon examination of the loan applications, both the comments of the applicant's bank and expert opinions by chambers and professional associations will be considered. If the project envisaged is technology-orientated, the governmental agency responsible for technology transfer must be consulted.

This program not only acknowledges investment costs as unconditionally eligible for financial assistance, but also the corresponding requirements regarding working capital. These modalities make sense when one considers that especially in the service sector there are new businesses which have correspondingly high funding requirements (cf. *Goldschmidt* 1985, p. 85).

The LKB makes some loan grants dependent upon the applicant simultaneously applying for an ERP loan or equity assistance, if possible. "This condition, applied in practice by the LKB in the majority of all loan promises, highlights again the fact that regional funding is only subsidiary to federal funding" (*Goldschmidt* 1985, p. 85, translated by W.H.).

In the period 1977 to 1984, a total of 19000 applications with a credit volume comprising approx. 1.1 billion DM granted from the LKB Program 1.

Although the sum of loan promises for a further 6351 applications granted in the years 1985 and 1986, amounting to a total of 374 million DM (cf. LKB (ed.) 1982 ff.), is still at a relatively high level, the share of start-up loans within all the LKB Small Business Pro- grams decreases in favor of the technology programs (see Table 3).

4. Equity assistances for setting-up

4.1. Equity assistance loans, DAB

On principle, equity assistance (capital owned) is granted to the person intending to set up business as repayable capital borrowed; the legal claim for repayment of the capital does, however, take second place behind the claims of any other creditors. This waiver of priority is also highly significant in case legal enforcement measures are taken against the company (cf. *Goldschmidt* 1985, p. 90). It is therefore a case of a "liability capital of lower priority" which, from the point of view of third party creditors, may be considered as capital owned under liability without restrictions, thus taking on the function of "risk capital" (cf. DAB (ed.), Annual Report 1986, p. 57) and extending the liability basis.

At the same time the credit rating of the company increases. The reason: Apart from the personal liability of the applicant and his/her spouse, no other credit securities are required. Even the material values obtained through equity assistance funds can be used by the applicant at his sole discretion, and they may also be used without any restriction for securing further bank credits (cf. *Brost* 1980, p. 41). Furthermore, the person starting up in business does not have to cope with the standard interest burden and, above all, with capital repayments.

Finally, the equity assistance loan (in contrast to publicly promoted capital interests) does not impair the entrepreneurial independence of the founder, because the lender does not have a voting right despite of his acceptance of liability and is, therefore, not shareholder (cf. *Goldschmidt* 1985, p. 90).

Table 3:
Splitting-up of the Loan Promises (in mio DM) into Special Programs within the LKB Small Business Program

year	foundings	technology-orientated foundings	promotion of technology	promotion of environment
1982	142.9	---	---	---
1983	242.2	---	---	---
1984*	237.5	7.5	26.2	13.5
1985	188.7	11.5	127.1	11.1
1986	185.3	11.5	220.1	11.9
1987	167.1	10.3	243.9	12.2
1988	187.2	12.5	250.1	32.3

*In order to give a new structure to the promotion of the economy, the programs concerning promotion of technology and protection of environment have been set up in 1984.

Source: Landeskreditbank Baden-Württemberg (ed.), Annual Reports 1983, 1984, 1986 and 1988.

Table 4:
Quantitative Development of the Equity Assistance Program (EAP)

year	loan volume total	loan volume for Baden-Württemberg
1980	95.0 mio DM	16.5 mio DM = 17.4 %
1981	78.2 mio DM	15.2 mio DM = 19.4 %
1982	95.4 mio DM	21.0 mio DM = 22.0 %
1983	367.4 mio DM	71.8 mio DM = 19.5 %
1984	466.6 mio DM	86.2 mio DM = 18.5 %
1985	471.5 mio DM	93.2 mio DM = 19.8 %
1986	481.3 mio DM	112.2 mio DM = 23.3 %
1987	496.9 mio DM	121.8 mio DM = 24.5 %
1988	519.4 mio DM	124.7 mio DM = 24.0 %

Source: Deutsche Ausgleichsbank (ed.), Annual Reports 1980 ff.

The importance of this program in the eyes of anyone intending to set up in business is shown by an empirical survey which demonstrated that every second business start-up would not have been possible without the equity assistance program (cf. *Hunsdiek/May-Strobl* 1987, p. 133).

In detail, the following provisions apply (cf. DBA (ed.), Programs ..., pp. 3-5):

Projects supported/appropriation:
In the field of commercial economy and in the professions, assistance is available for the following:
- setting up an independent business,
- take-over of existing company,
- active interest;
  of 500 million DM granted in 1987 by way of equity assistance loans, about 55 % accounted for starting new companies, 40 % was for take-overs of existing companies and 5 % for active interests (cf. *Schiller* 1987, p. 2);
- (follow-up)investments in connection with setting up new businesses within 2 years from the beginning of business activities, but only if equity capital assistance was granted already.

The latter provision might be seen as a virtual challenge to apply for equity assistance during the initial phases of the business, in advance, so to speak (namely with a view on possible capital requirements occuring 2 years after the start-up) (cf. *Goldschmidt* 1985, p. 92).

Entitlement:
Individuals must not be older than 50 years and show evidence of professional and business qualifications as far as normally required for practicing within this profession. On principle, the DAB requires the comments of independent and competent agencies (e.g., professional associations, experts with public recognition, auditors, etc.) with regard to these qualifications and the economic prospects of success of the intended business venture. The reason for handling the applications restrictively lies in the fact that the DAB, by granting unsecured equity assistance loans with low priority liability, accepts a higher credit risk (cf. *Brost* 1980, p. 45 f.).

Judging from experience, about 10 % of all applications are turned down, because substantial doubts regarding either the qualification of the applicant or his prospects of success have arisen (cf. *Schiller* 1987, p. 3). The proportion of women as business founders applying for equity assistance has been relatively constant at 23 % since 1982 (cf. DAB (ed.), Annual Report 1986, p. 48).

Terms of equity loans:

- amount: Capital owned may be increased with equity assistance up to 40 % of the total costs eligible for support (assessment basis = investment sum plus goods in stock); since the person setting up in business is expected to have a minimum of 15 % of the amount required, the equity assistance may therefore be as high as 25 % of the assessment basis. Assistance is also limited to a maximum sum of DM 300,000.
- interest: The interest rate agreed upon when granting the equity assistance loan remains fixed until the end of the 10th year; it is reduced with federal funds as follows:

in the 1st and 2nd year:	interest-free
in the 3rd year:	2 %
in the 4th year:	3 %
in the 5th year:	5 %
in the 6th to 10th year:	standard commercial interest rate (approx. 9.5 - 10.5 % in 1990)
in the 11th to 20th year:	new fixation of interest rate for remaining term of loan.

The interest includes the bank charges (with the exception of any handling fees).

- handling fees:	2 %, to be paid by applicant;
- sum paid out:	100 %;
- duration:	20 years (repayable at the latest when the applicant reaches the age of 70);
- redemption:	after 10 redemption-free years, in 20 equal 6-monthly instalments.

Early repayments are possible, maintaining a 3-months period of notice ending March 31st and September 30th of any one year. In case of early repayment within the first 7 years, half the interest paid by the Federation during the first 5 years must be repaid. This provision does not apply to repayment in connection with the relinquishment of the independent existence.

Criticism: If a "pocket effect" is suspected afterwards, because the loan was repaid within the first 7 years, it is hard to see why the subsidy (which was evidently paid wrongfully in terms of assistance policies) should not be paid back in full instead of only half (cf. also *Goldschmidt* 1985, p. 94).

- securities: personal liability on the part of the applicant and his/her spouse; no further securities!

Application procedure:
Applications may be submitted to the DAB via any credit institute. "During application, the applicant's bank confirms -by way of an accompanying letter addressed to the DAB - that the intended business could not be started without an equity assistance loan or that it could otherwise only be started with great difficulties. When evaluating such letters of confirmation issued by the applicant's bank, the DAB recognizes that such comments may also be influenced by subjective considerations, whereby the bank's own interests in spreading the risk involved may play a substantial part" (*Goldschmidt* 1985, p. 94, translated by W.H.).

Time limit:
Originally, the equity assistance program was to be discontinued after December 31st, 1988. Through a budget resolution by the federal government, it was extended for three years; applications may therefore be submitted before December 31st, 1991.

The quantitative development of the equity assistance program is shown in Table 4. As can be seen in the table, about 20 % or more of the total annual volume of the equity assistance programs have been granted to new business ventures in Baden-Württemberg in each year since 1981. What is furthermore remarkable is the "drop-out rate" of the EAP loans: If one adds up all the enterprises supported by means of equity assistance since 1986, one finds that "by numbers, precisely 1074 enterprises have dropped out from a total of 46000 companies supported by end 1986. This figure corresponds to a rate of 2.3 %. With 2.1 %, the drop-out rate with reference to the total loan allocation volume during the 8-year period recorded is similarly low" (DAB (ed.), Annual Report 1986, p. 57). These figures certainly convey an over-optimistic picture, because many of the 46000 companies receiving funds have not yet lived through their first, usually decisive, 5 years, having been established only recently. In order to obtain somewhat more realistic drop-out figures, we suggest to look only at those companies which were founded as early as 1984. Of the new businesses established in 1984 which received equity assistance, exactly 5.4 % (with reference to the number of businesses founded) or 6.4 % (with reference to the amounts subsidized) had declared their insolvency by the end of 1988 (cf. DAB (ed.), Annual Report 1988, p. 23f.).

4.2. Participation capital from capital participation companies

The term "capital participation company" (CPC) means "special finance institutes participating with capital contributions to companies not capable of issuing securities" (*Vallenthin* 1976, c. 1021, translated by W.H.). Especially smaller and medium sized firms and family businesses are supposed to be given the opportunity to procure their own capital.

The connecting link with the loan programs is as follows:
- "From the outset, participations take place only for an exactly defined and contractually agreed period of time; thereafter, they must be purchased back by the beneficiary *at the nominal value*. Also, the largest share of the participatory remuneration, in the form of a percentage independent from profits, is payable on the capital deployed, i.e. similar to interest. That is why this funding instrument also displays some essential characteristics of outside financing, although the participations imply represent capital owned from the point of view of legal liability" (*Goldschmidt* 1985, p. 155, translated by W.H.).
- The extended endowment of medium sized businesses with liability capital also entails an indirect assistance regarding the possibilities to take up credits, since the readiness of the banks to grant loans largely depends on the capital cover of the creditor (cf. *Goldschmidt* 1985, p. 155).

The following provisions for participation financing (from the Mittelständische Beteiligungsgesellschaft, Baden- Württemberg, for instance) apply:

Projects supported/appropriation:
Financing practical projects, such as:
a) (partial) financing for investments in buildings and machinery,
b) (partial) financing of innovations,

c) (partial) replacement of a "cumbersome partner", as well as pay-outs after the distribution of an estate among heirs.
The project may be started, but not yet completed.

Entitlement:
Trainees in small and medium sized businesses of the commercial economy, whereby the business must be *un*encumbered by any capital participation companies or any other finance institute; (no "free professions"). Companies with a turnover exceeding 100 million DM or with a staff of more than 499 people are not eligible. The company must have existed for at least 3 years.

Terms of participation:
- amount: from DM 100,000 up to DM 1 million, but not more than the company's equity shown in the balance sheet (i.e. maximum 50 % participation).
- duration of participation: max. 10 years; the beneficiary is regularly given the unilateral right to terminate the participation in whole or in part following a 12-months' period of notice.
- costs (terms and conditions of the Mittelständische Beteiligungsgesellschaft):
  a) handling fee: 1 % of participation, due upon application; following refusal or revocation of the application, one half of the handling fee is refunded.
  b) The costs of the participation, amounting to max. 10 % p.a. of the participation sum during the term of the agreement, are broken down as follows:
    - fixed remuneration of 8 % and
    - profit-dependent remuneration of 2 %, provided that the annual profit accumulated exceeds a contractually agreed minimum sum (cf. *Goldschmidt* 1985, p. 168).
    - liability for loss: in case of bankruptcy or in case of legal settlement with creditors, the participation partakes in the loss. As a rule, the participation is deemed to be the contribution of a sleeping partner.
    - securities: none, except the acceptance of guarantee by the owner/partner and their spouses. Securities remain freely available for credits.

Application procedure:
The application can be submitted informally to the Mittelständische Beteiligungsgesellschaft Baden-Württemberg, GmbH.

Table 5 shows the development of the publicly supported participations of newly established businesses in Baden-Württemberg.

5. Non-repayable subsidies for new businesses

Besides non-repayable subsidies granted by the Federal Commercial Office under certain conditions for consultancy fees incurred in setting up business, the non-repayable allowances mentioned here specifically include those for establishing a technology-orientated business (TOU). The pilot model "Promotion of Technology-Orientated New Businesses" as an example for non-repayable subsidies may be worth a closer look.

Projects supported/appropriation:
Eligible for assistance are innovative projects which

- aim at developing new products, processes and technical services up to the time of launching in the market, followed by the marketing of the above products/services,
- require substantial development expenses with significant technical risks,
- the applicant, owing to insufficent capital cover, is unable to develop and realize commercially,
- are intended to be manufactured entirely by the applicant (in case of product development) and for which the decisive machines, appliances, devices, components or materials are manufactured (in case of process development) and which, in the case of services, are to be offered on the free market,
- are aimed at regions where certain technology information centers have been established. The restriction regarding locality does not apply to:
  - innovative projects in which micro-electronics are a decisive functional component,
  - innovative projects within certain fields of biotechnology,
  - innovative projects in up to 15 selected founder centers or technology parks,
  - innovative projects in phases 2 and 3, in the financing of which risk capital enterprises participate with a minimum of 25 %.

Entitlement:

- persons intending to establish a technology-orientated commercial business, or

Table 5:
Development of Participations of Newly Established Businesses in Baden-Württemberg

year	foundings	technology-orientated foundings
1978	1.3 mio DM	
1979	11.3 mio DM	
1980	15.6 mio DM	
1981	2.8 mio DM	
1982	2.5 mio DM	
1983	1.3 mio DM	
1984	2.1 mio DM	4.3 mio
1985	2.3 mio DM	3.8 mio
1986	1.0 mio DM	4.9 mio
1987	1.4 mio DM	3.7 mio
1988	0.6 mio DM	2.5 mio

Source: Mittelständische Beteiligungsgesellschaft Baden-Württemberg GmbH (ed.), Annual Reports 1978 ff.

Table 6:
Simultaneous Use of Several Financial Assistance Programs for One Particular Project

Needed volume: 1 mio DM = 100 %

Personally owned equity	Equity Assistance Program	ERP-Start-Up Program	LKB-Program 1
150,000 DM = 15 %	250,000 DM = 25 %	300,000 DM = 30 %	300,000 DM = 30 %

Public financial assistance total: 850,000 DM = 85 %

- technology-orientated commercial companies
  - not older than 3 years,
  - with a staff of less than 10,
  - not majority-owned by third parties (legal entities or individuals).

One or more of the persons participating in the business applying for assistance must have the specialist technological knowledge necessary for realizing the project. These persons must have a share of at least 25 % in the business and they are required to dedicate most of their working efforts to the business to be established in phases 2 and 3.

Scope/type of grant:
- As long as a concept for the innovative project, amenable to evaluation, has as yet not been prepared (phase I), subsidies by way of non-repayable grants of up to 90 %, but not more than DM 54000, may be paid for work involved in drafting documentations amenable to evaluation.
- Subsidies by way of non-repayable grants of up to 75 %, but not more than DM 900,000, may be paid for financing innovative projects in phase 2 (research and development). Bank credits needed for financing these projects may be secured in individual cases by risk participation of up to 50 %, but not more than DM 150,000.
- Bank credits needed for financing expenses incurred for production facilities and market introduction (phase 3) may be secured in individual cases by risk participation of up to 80 %, but not more than DM 1.6 million. The applicant's bank must be prepared to grant at least two redemption-free years for such credits.

The risk participations extend over a maximum period of 10 years. They are only granted for credits for which no securities (e.g. financed objects) sufficient for a long-term credit can be provided. If the DAB accepts risk participation in phases 2 or 3, they are entitled to receive a one-off flat-rat handling fee of 0.75 % of the participation sum.

Application procedure:
Applications for subsidies may be submitted until December 31st, 1988. Applications for risk participations (phases 2 and 3) must be addressed to the DAB by the applicant's bank. The final decision

regarding the grant is taken by the BMFT (Federal Ministry of Research and Technology) following the recommendation by the competent technology information center or by the DAB.

6. Cumulation possibilities

Finally, it is worth asking up to which degree the *simultaneous* use of several financial assistance programs is possible for one particular project of starting up a new business. For example, we need a volume of 1 mio. DM for establishing a new business. The person setting up in business is expected to have, by own means (equity), a minimum of 15 % of the amount required, i.e. 150,000 DM. Then the capital owned may be increased with equity assistance loans up to 40 % (= 400,000 DM) of the total amount; therefore the founder is able to get 250,000 DM from the equity assistance program of DAB. Another 300,000 DM (maximum amount) can be provided from the ERP Start-up Program and the remaining 300,000 DM could be financed by loans of the LKB-Program I.

Table 6 shows this admissible *combination* (i.e., simultaneous use) of several financial assistance programs for one particular project of starting up a new business (cf. *Goldschmidt* 1985, S. 100). As can be seen in the table, the total volume (1 mio. DM) needed for starting up a new business could be financed - at best - up to an extent of 85 % by publicly promoted loans.

References

Brost, O., Das Eigenkapitalhilfeprogramm in der Praxis, in: M. E. *Kamp* (ed.), Mittelstandspolitische Akzente 1981, , Göttingen 1980, p. 39 ff.

Deutsche Ausgleichsbank (ed.), Jahresberichte (Annual Reports), 1982 ff.

Deutsche Ausgleichsbank (ed.), Kreditinstitut des Bundes für Mittelstand, Umweltschutz, soziale Aufgaben (Federal Credit Institute ...), Vol. 1

Deutsche Ausgleichsbank (ed.), Finanzierungshilfen für gewerbliche Existenzgründungen (Financial Assistance ...), Vol. 3

Deutsche Ausgleichsbank (ed.), Programme, Richtlinien, Merkblätter (Programs ...), (2/1990), situation as per February 1990

Goldschmidt, Th., Öffentliche Kredithilfen im Rahmen der Mittelstands- und Regionalpolitik in Baden-Württemberg, Konzeption und Praxis der Programme zugunsten der gewerblichen Wirtschaft, Doctoral Dissertation, Freiburg i.Br. 1985

Häussler, W., Neue staatliche Finanzierungshilfen für Unternehmen, 2 Volumes, Kissing 1988

Hunsdiek, D./*May-Strobl*, E., Gründungsfinanzierung durch den Staat - Fakten, Erfolg und Wirkung -, Stuttgart 1987
Landeskreditbank Baden-Württemberg, (LKB), (ed.), Geschäftsberichte (Annual Reports), 1982, 1983, 1986, 1988

Mittelständische Beteiligungsgesellschaft Baden-Württemberg GmbH (ed.), Geschäftsberichte (Annual Reports), 1978 ff.

Mittelständische Beteiligungsgesellschaft Baden-Württemberg GmbH (ed.), Richtlinien der geförderten Beteiligungsfinanzierung (Guidelines ...), situation as per 1 January 1990

Wirtschaftsmacht Mittelstand: Leistung, Gewinne, Investitionen, in: impulse, 6/1986, (no author given), p. 6 ff.

Schiller, R., Financing Aids for Entrepreneurs Starting New Business, Paper presented at the 17th European Small Business Seminar, Genova 1987

Vallenthin, W., Kapitalbeteiligungsgesellschaften, in: H. E. *Büschgen* (ed.), Handwörterbuch der Finanzwirtschaft, Stuttgart 1976, c. 1021-1028

The Governmental Policy of Small and Medium-sized Enterprises in Japan

Eiji Ogawa

1. A short history of the SMEs (small and medium-sized enterprises) policy of Japan

Japan is called a country of SMEs, because the share of SMEs in the Japanese economy is so high that no other advanced country can claim the same position as Japan. According to current statistics based on the definition of Japanese government, SMEs belonging to the manufacturing sector amounted to 99.9 % of the total number of establishments in 1981. The same thing happened in the tertiary sector of businesses in Japan. It is well-known that the Japanese economy consists of big businesses and SMEs. Additionally it is said that they often co-operate with each other by utilizing a sub-contracting system. Since after World War II, Japanese government has recognized the importance of SMEs not only in the large number of such businesses but also in the relationship with big businesses. This was the reason why the government enacted laws which intended to promote SMEs.

First of all, the government established the Small Business Administration under the law enacted in 1948. This was only three years after the end of the war. Three governmental banks were ready to support financing for SMEs up to 1951. One more governmental institution, namely the Public Corporation of Providing Credit Guarantee for SMEs, was established in 1958. Since then, these four organizations have engaged in financing capital for the SMEs which suffered from the keen shortage of capital. The government strengthened co-operative organization by law, first in 1948 and then after revision in 1952. The later one aimed at overcoming the keen competition among SMEs. This one was revised again in 1957 and was called the Law for Groups of SMEs. It is still in effect even now.

Along with such measures as financing and the promotion of cooperative activities among SMEs, the government enacted several laws for SMEs such as the Law of Promoting the Rationalization of SMEs (1952), the Law of Protecting Subcontractors from the Delay of Payment (1956) and the Law of Department Store (1956) which was expected to protect smaller retailers from the aggressive activities undertaken by department stores. Although Japanese SMEs policy in 1950s covered such areas as mentioned, it is said that the governmental measures adopted were rather fragmentary. It was in the early 1960s that the SMEs policy of Japanese government was systematized as to show real effectiveness.

The government decided to amalgamate diverse governmental measures and to enact a systematized law for SMEs then. This law, which was legislated in 1963, declared that the importance of SMEs did not change at all corresponding to both economic development and the betterment of people's living. In order to realize such declaration, the government in the same year enacted or revised the laws such as the Law of the Corporation of Investing Capital in SMEs to Modernize Equipments and so on. The White Paper of SMEs was firstly published in 1964. Since then, everybody has had the opportunity to access to detailed information about SMEs.

The SMEs of Japan were obliged to adapt to the tendency of trade liberalization in the 1960s, because the government started the liberalizing scheme of international trade and exchange, which was requested from not only advanced countries but also LDCs. During the 1960s, the SMEs of Japan had two courses which were caused by the movement of liberalization. One was the course of high growth and the other was the decline of exports to advanced countries, which affected to the light industry. The former benefited fully from the laws enacted in 1963, while the latter hoped to find a way to survive by shifting from out-dated products to modern ones with support by the laws mentioned above.

Although the Japanese economy grew fast in the 1960s, nobody forecasted what happened in the 1970s. The yen appreciation and the Oil Shocks I and II brought troubles to Japanese SMEs. The government provided SMEs with the measures to cope with the emergent condition. First of all, the government made clear the direction of SMEs in the 1970s. It was called strengthening "knowledge-intensiveness" in the operation of SMEs. The government stressed the importance of developing new technology and products, which resulted in the development of a new market. The Law of Promoting Modernization of SMEs was revised toward the newly decided direction in 1973. As for the textile industry which was losing competitiveness, the government revised the Law of Temporary Measures for the Structural Reformation in Specified Textile Industry in 1974 (which was legislated first in 1967). In order to promote the movement of "knowledge-intensiveness", the government established the Center for Nurturing Research-oriented Enterprises in 1975. The Law of Temporary Measures for Promoting the Shift from a Stagnant Business Field was enacted in 1976, and aimed at promoting SMEs to move easily from their stagnant business field.

The government also dramatically switched a regional policy. The new policy emphasized the importance of considering the significance of a regional economy. A regional economy has its own culture and tradition which are worth being kept. For this reason, the government legislated the Law of Promoting the Industry which Engaged in the Production of Traditonal and Artistic Products. The Law of Temporary Measures for the SMEs in a Producing Area, enacted in 1979, intended to overcome difficulties caused by Yen appreciation, by using measures such as manpower, new product and new market development.

The basic policy for SMEs of Japan, taken care by the government in the 1980s, considered SMEs as a vital majority. Strengthening employee's welfare and promoting business activities of SMEs in a regional economy were targets to be adopted by the government. Based upon the direction designated, the government first opened a College of SMEs in 1980. The information center for SMEs was established on a prefectural basis. In 1983, the Law of Technopolis was enacted in order to develop areas of research-oriented firms. The Law of Temporary Measures to Develop New Technology by SMEs, en-acted in 1985, hoped to promote technological development among SMEs and their cooperatives. Because of the yen appreciation in the late 1980s, the government strongly hopes to nurture new servicing industries which will contribute to the development of a new domestic market. In summary, the SMEs policy, which is set up by Japanese government, is now focused on nurturing highly competitive firms in the world.

2. Internationalization and Japanese SMEs

The liberalization of international trade and exchange started in 1960. The government issued the Report of the Outline of

Liberalizing International Trade and Exchange. After the issuance, Japan's participation in the OECD (1964) took place. Also there occurred the reduction of tariffs from 1964 to 1967. The liberalization of capital investment to Japan started in 1967 and the liberalization of capital investment from Japan to a foreign country in 1969. During 1960s, the content of exports from Japan changed drastically. Export figures declined in the light industry while they climbed in the heavy industry. The SMEs engaged in production in the light industry in the U.S. and Europe in the 1960s. Hongkong, Taiwan and South Korea deprived Japanese SMEs of markets such products as umbrellas, chemicals, shoes, knives and forks, apparel and so on. The SMEs which suffered to lose export market, changed the direction of business activities from export to a domestic market. They improved their products by adjusting to tastes of Japanese consumers. Some SMEs changed their business field and entered into a new field belonging to the heavy industry as subcontractors. As for the import from LDCs, although there were shocks in some industries, the domestic SMEs of Japan were successful in coping with the competition from LDCs in general.

The direct investment to and from Japan was not so large even though the liberalizing scheme was adopted. The direct investment to Japan amounted to 485 cases and 1,650 million dollars while the direct investment from Japan reached at 2,671 cases and 3,004 million dollars by the end of 1969. In the beginning of the 1970s, the overseas direct investment from Japan skyrocketed, but it was crushed by Oil Shock I. But after 1978, investment was revitalized.

Facing to the internationalization of trade and exchange, it was thought that SMEs of Japan had to modernize their operations. For this reason, the government improved policy measures to reform industrial structure. The Law of Promoting the Modernization of SMEs (revised in 1963) was revised again (in 1967) from the modernization of an individual firm to group modernization. The law was again revised in the 1970s. In 1974, the law stressed the promotion of quality enhancement, new product development, and the development of new technology. Those activities were summarized as being intensifying a knowledge basis. Furthermore, the entry into a new business field was added to this law in 1975. The revised law expected for SMEs to be competitive in the world. But some exporting SMEs had fatal damage from yen appreciation and the Oil Shock I and II. Therefore, the government proposed and enacted several measures like the Law of Temporary Measures for

SMEs to Counteract to the Preferential Tariffs Given to LDCs (1971), the Law of the Temporary Measures for SMEs to Cope with the Difficulties Followed by International Adjustment (yen floating) (1971), the Law of Temporary Measures for Promoting Shift from a Stagnant Business Field (1976), the Law of Temporary Measures for the SMEs Suffered from Yen Appreciation (1978), the Law of Temporary Measures for the SMEs in a Specified Depressed Area in 1978 and the Law of Temporary Measures for the SMEs in a Producing Area (1979). The government hoped that badly affected SMEs would be relieved by the laws mentioned above.

The yen appreciation did not stop in late 1980s. Export-oriented SMEs were hit severely by this appreciation. The government decided to provide them with two measures such as the Law of Temporary Measures for the Specified SMEs Intending the Shift from a Stagnant Business Field (1986) and the Law of Temporary Measures for the SMEs in a Specified Area (1986). Amidst free trade, Japanese government can no longer protect SMEs. All the government can do is to accelerate the speed of both structural reform and strengthening competitiveness of SMEs concerned. The firm which does not have the willingness to excel will be squeezed out from any market.

With respect to the internationalization of SMEs, the government now provides SMEs with diverse services such as the dissemination of information, introduction to an appropriate partner abroad, holding an international exhibition, the promotion of imports, the survey of a foreign market and so on.

3. The governmental policy for the SMEs engaging in textile production

The textile industry of Japan was the number one industry in production and export before World War II. As soon as the war was over, the Japanese government started to plan reviving production of textile products. The government completed this plan of rebuilding the textile industry of Japan in 1948. But the industry suffered heavily from the depression following the end of the Korean War. The Ministry of International Trade and Industry (MITI) ordered an output restriction for spinning companies in 1952. In the same year, the government first enacted the law which permitted SMEs to organize a cartel group in order to overcome a depression. This law was revised in 1954 and 1958. It intended to control production capacity by requiring registration of equipments and forbidding purchase of a new equipment. It is now still applied only to some textile products such as the following: cotton cloth, woolen cloth, silk cloth, hemp-cloth, towels, knitted cloth, knitted lace, twined yarn, and woven cloth with narrow breadth.

The textile industry consists of three parts such as "up stream", "mid stream" and "down stream". The "up stream" covers spinning, the "mid stream" occupies the weaving and knitting stage, while the "down stream" covers apparel production. SMEs belong mainly to the "mid-stream" and "down stream" parts.

Regarding governmental regulation, the textile industry continued the restriction of equipments corresponding to environmental changes. The special law for the textile industry was legislated in 1956 and stayed in effect up to 1964. It was expected that the specified industry could export orderly through regulation of production capacity. The law just mentioned above was broken down into three parts. The first part was for the spinning industry, the second one for the weaving and knitting industry and the third one for the industry of synthetic fibers. The SMEs which were operating in the "mid stream" started to modernize business operations supported by the Law of Promoting the Modernization of SMEs (enacted in 1963). The new law which aimed at strengthening international competitiveness was enacted in 1967. It was the law of structural reformation in the textile industry, by disposing out-dated equipments, modernizing them and promoting the cooperative operations among SMEs. The structural reformation was accelerated by both the Special Law for the Textile Industry and the Law of Promoting the Modernization of SMEs (revised furthermore in 1969).

The Japanese government had an agreement with the U.S. concerning the export of textile products from Japan in 1971. In order to compensate the hardship brought by the above agreement, the government arranged relief measures for the textile industry concerned. They lasted from 1971 to 1974. The government strengthened the disposition of out-dated equipments, financed long-term capital, increased the amount of credit guarantee, funded money for promoting the industry and extended the term of repayment, then.

Japanese industry set the future direction which strengthened "knowledge intensiveness" in the beginning of the 1970s. The textile industry of Japan was no exception. The new Textile Law came out in 1974, stressing the importance of vertical cooperation. This law was revised in order to activate the apparel industry in 1979. Furthermore, the law was extended from 1984 to 1989, adding to the promotion of technological development. The Council of Textile Industry affiliating to MITI is now discussing the future direction of the industry which is challenged by rapid yen appreciation and a sharp increase of imports. The government hopes strongly that Japanese SMEs in the textile industry will be able to compete with any foreign competitor. The governmental measures which are now being debated will be along the line of those mentioned above.

4. Outlines of the current policy for SMEs

The SMEs policy of Japan consists of the following parts: (1) aids to the structural change which is carried by SMEs, corresponding to the structural change by industry as a whole, (2) strengthening resources for SMEs corresponding to environmental changes, (3) strengthening the infrastructure for SMEs, by which they are able to grow steadily, and (4) making sure of the autonomous growth of very small firms.

Aids to the structural change of SMEs are broken down into four sections. The first one relates to planning governmental measures. The second one engages in the promotion of local SMEs. The third one is responsible for taking care of subcontractors. The last one promotes the internationalization of SMEs.

As for strengthening the resources of SMEs, there are three focal points such as the enhancement of technological capability, strengthening information dissemination, and the promotion of manpower development.

In order to strengthen infrastructure for SMEs, the government takes care of many measures such as financing, tax exemption, promotion of co-operative activities, consultation, the modernization of equipments and so on.

The governmental measures for very small firms broadly cover businesses from manufacturing to retailing and servicing. Measures cover management improvement, the modernization of equipments, the system of mutual insurances and consultation. As mentioned above, the government is interested in the activation of newly developing servicing businesses. It is hoped that these businesses grow fast and tap a new domestic market which offsets the imbalance of international trade.

5. Summary

The governmental policy for SMEs changed three times after World War II. From the end of war to the end of the 1950s, the government intended to limit excess competition among SMEs and to modernize management and equipments. The governmental measures started to change in the beginning of the 1960s corresponding to the direction of liberalizing trade and exchange. The SMEs which were hit hard by liberalization were relieved by several government measures. Especially, the textile industry was a main target for applying relief measures. This is the reason why this paper picks up the applying of the textile industry of Japan.

Since after 1970, the government has stressed the concept of "knowledge-intensiveness". It emphasized the activities of developing a new product and a new market. Because of the swift change of technology, SMEs were expected to be innovators in the beginning of the 1980s. The government arranged measures which promoted the innovativeness of SMEs. Such direction of the governmental action still remains the same. The government will help SMEs which determine to take the course towards becoming an internationally more competitive firm in the future.

References

Association of Surveys for SMEs, The Future of New Textile Industry, 1977

Association of Surveys for SMEs, The Outline of the Governmental Measures for SMEs, 1987

Small Business Administration, White Paper of SMEs, Tokyo, yearly

Takizawa, K., (ed.), Foreign Investment by SMEs, Tokyo (Yuhikaku) 1982

Tatsumi, N./*Yamamoto*, J., (ed.), Reexamination of the Governmental Policy for SMEs, Tokyo (Yuhikaku) 1983

Tatsumi, N./*Satoh*, Y., (ed.), Introduction to SMEs, Tokyo (Yuhikaku) 1988

Planning Efficiency as a Basis of Entrepreneurial Decisions-Common Elements in the Light of Divergent Economic Policy

Ralf-Bodo Schmidt

1. The thesis

The leading motive of our exchange of ideas is called: Protectionism or liberalization. This is primarily an economic problem from a general economic point of view concerning international economic relationships. But also the individual company is touched, because its decisions of goal attainment referring to products, result and liquidity as well as of goal achievement are exposed to different strict conditions.

Here and today, I cannot report of the resultant perplexity of special industries or individual companies. Instead of that, I consider it advisable to lecture some fundamental comments, which should be the task of the science of business management regarding the importance of the problem.

2. Fundamental terms

(1) At first the term *"planning"* should be explained because it has a different meaning in the relevant sciences.

- From the view of *economic policy*, planning means in the case of "Protectionism" the rationing of product quantities with corresponding restrictions for the company's achievement of selected and imposed result and liquidity goals. In the case of "liberalism" this term is just an empty formula.

- In the modern *science of business management*, based on the decision theory, planning has another signification. It is the decision preparation in the sense of information gaining, search of alternatives, etc.. There might be a gradual, but no specific difference between planning in "protectionism" and planning in"liberalism".

(2) Secondly the term *"efficiency"* - in the sense of rational behaviour - is worthy to be considerated.

- From the view of the *"economic policy"* (as a theoretical discipline), any explanation is unnecessary in the case of "liberalism". However, it is very problematic for protectionism, particularly as this is part of the States' economic philosophy what I cannot comment.

- From the side of *"business economics"*, the definition is nearly trivial. Efficient action requires the best possible achievement of extreme and limited goals from the manager. Thereby - regarding the role which is expected from him - he must deeply regret "protectionism", but he has also to take it as a challenge.

Without doubt, interdisciplinary relations are existing and the experience teaches us that the struggle for efficiency is motivated differently in different economic systems.

3. Important details

(1) It seems suitable to me to make the following assumptions:
- In every situation *exists* one rational decision.
- Rational decisions have the *best* result.

However, these assumptions are only valid with the restriction that rationality cannot be observed without fail in successful decisions and at last cannot be realized completely, even if only subjective rationality is required.

(2) These fundamental statements have to be explained in more details.

a) Planning mainly consists of a series of different information operations as there are information gaining and processing as well as information storage and transmission. Quality and success of planning depend on the carefulness of the realized information processes. Overcoming the imperfection of information is one of the essential planning problems. Whilst uncompleteness and indefiniteness of information can be reduced by gaining additional and more precise information with regard to cost/benefit reflections, the uncertainty of information, which is caused by the indeterminateness of reality as well as by the lacking knowledge of reality, represents a planning dilemma. Planning has to pay attention to this fact what means that certainty itself is a criterion to judge the planning rationality. The danger that realized effects of decisions differ from the planned consequences - what is called the planning *risk* - is itself an object of planning and decision. Insofar it can be more rational to prefer a less effective but certain alternative to a more effective but risky possibility.

Considering the planning risk, the planning complexity is completed by a further component. Thereby, the task of planning is primarily to overcome complexity by appropriate measures of information gaining and processing. Evaluating alternatives as a kind of information *processing* is less difficult by criteria of rationality, because these evaluations are various logical transformations based on models and methods, the formal rationality of these is well-known in the science. However, their use depends subjectively on the fact that these methods are known and practicable as well as from an objective view on the importance of the decision problem.

It is more difficult to analyse the rationality of information *gaining* and *searching processes* because these cannot be completely analysed on a logical basis what represents the difference to those of process results. However, in connection with satisfying rules, criteria can be found which enable a graduation of rationality. It might be rational behaviour, if the search for alternatives is finished when one alternative guarantees a satisfying goal achievement. Insofar, verifications can be realized with the help of economic analysis referring to the loss of time. With that planning has to be formed in an economic manner to reconcile cost and benefits. Rational planning is goal-oriented. As the company goals - if they are chosen and not forced by the economic order, like it is the case for the classifying liquidity goal - are a result of decisions, the rationality of processes of goal attainment has also to be tested. Thereby it has to be questioned if the process and the chosen alternatives - that means the *company goals* and with that the *planning goals* - correspond to reasonable criteria. In the individual case, it is an independent and multi-personal problem of the company, but both processes are *formally* comparable, nevertheless, goal attainment and planning cannot be separated, they work into each other. If planning is not based on operational goals, because they cannot be followed up, measured or there is not time-orientation, which represent three basic conditions, they will be influenced - according to experience - parallel to and by the planning progress, and impressing the process they were concretized, operationalized and, if necessary, adapted to the realization possibilities. These interdependences of *goal attainment* and *planning* are insofar important, as the compatibility of goals has not only to be judged with meta-goals, but also their formulation which is relevant for planning represents a necessity. Therefore, *formal rationality* is only sufficient for planning if the goals are fixed or if their modification is out of competence of the involved person; in the other case planning has to be analysed referring to *substantial* rationality.

This consequence is emphasized by the fact that goals and goal achievement are often connected with various - and also undesired - results which cannot be ignored by planning. Therefore, the selection of goals and the identificaion of undesired results is also a criterion for rationality which, however, is strictly related to the subject because of restricted human qualities and imperfect information. Furthermore, the *subjective rationality* can be described by typical *preferences* which are related to content, extent, time and risk. A person which is involved in planning often prefers certain goals, alternatives, models and procedures by individual valuation what reduces complexity, because all elements of planning which do not correspond with the individual preferences are eliminated. In an extreme case planning can be given up because of time and cost reasons, and instead of that routine and ad hoc decisions will take place. According to that, conflict resolution in planning and decision situations by individual valuation is the contribution of preferences to the rationalization of planning which can only be identified - however not necessary accepted - by outstanding persons if the valuation is displayed. Interpersonal conflicts which are also located on the value level have to be separated from that. Insofar multi-personal planning can produce intransitive and with that from the logical view contradictory value orders what might already mean a lacking formal rationality. Overcoming such conflict situations, the behaviour of the "opponent" has to be integrated in the planning process and with that the rationality concept has to be enlarged by an additional dimension, like it is practiced in the models of the *game theory*. At last differences between the individual and the organization referring to the mentioned valuation are possible.

b) In connection with planning rationality, it has to be checked, if and in what respect rationality is observable and with that provable, what offers the classification in *objective* and *subjective* rationality. Apart from the fact that decisions came also into existence by irrational factors, it has to be considered the information level of the persons which are concerned with planning. A decider will be able to choose the best possible alternative if he is perfectly informed of all decision possibilities and of the present as well as future consequences of these; therefore, an outstanding person who is informed in like manner can check the rightness of the decision. As however, the assumption of perfect information is not realistic, a term of *objective* rationality, which is connected with that, has to be eliminated as unusable. According to this term, planning is rational, if - con- sidering the *entire* knowledge - the maximum is fixed in a definite situation. In a less strict interpretation, objective rationality can also be understood and used as choosing the best possible alternative on the basis of present available knowledge.

Purely personal qualities of the planning member, like the "volition", the "knowledge" and the "capability", are only considered in the case of *subjective rationality*; an individual decides rationally here, if it chooses the best alternative regarding to its individual information level. Herewith, the processes of information gaining and processing themselves are an object of decisions referring to completeness, definiteness and certainty of information. In this case - from the viewpoint of scientifically requested, intersubjective capability of being test - a control is insofar problematic as different persons regard and judge differently the same situation. Planning can be undoubtly subjective rational if it is done by a person with less knowledge though a planning unit with higher knowledge might judge it as not rational.

In connection with the conditions of the company planning the subjective rationality has to be put insofar in relativity as the goals and the value system of the company or the organization unit have to be taken into consideration. Elements and procedures of planning have to be made transparent and capable for control because of reasons of planning responsibility, what would correspond with *intersubjective* provable rationality, and with that it represents an approach to objective rationality as well as it might satisfy practical needs.

4. Conclusions

Entrepreneurial decisions which are preceded by planning as decision preparation represent always a "skill of possibles". This becomes more important when a decision situation demands more "dynamic". By all means, the question is which constellation produces more tension: Protectionism or liberalism? From the view point of the science of business management, an answer is not insofar necessary as the general instruments are prepared for both cases, all the more protectionism can be seen (without any academic doubt) as a speciality of "open markets": It is only the restriction of sales volumes, but with the connected consequences for result and liquidity.

From this view two strategies can be offered:

(1) *Defensivė Adaption.* Its mainpoints are chiefly located in the cost and liquidity *planning.*

(2) *Active Mobilization.* It is particularly directed on the variation of the product range and with that also to disclose new markets what implies the improvement of information providing in the planning process.

In both cases, the needs of leadership in the company have to be reflected. Hence, it follows in every case:

- Intensifying the sense of problem for the planning.

- All desisions, which are made, do not have their results today, but in an uncertain future. Uncertainty of the future requests quick adaptions, that means *decision quality* by solid planning and *decision rapidity.*

Paradox and Organization
- Liberalism and Conservatism in Organization -

Tamiki Kishida

1. Introduction

Since 1960, Contingency Theory, based on an open systems approach, has asserted that the fit between organization and environment leads to high performance. The concept of fit has also developed as follows. First, there was the selection approach which stressed the survival of the organization as the result of natural selection. For example, Aston Group found a strong relationship between size and organization structure (structuring of activities consisting of specialization, formalization and standardization). The second approach was interactional in that it emphasized the interaction between a situational factor and a dimension of organization structure. Representatives are J. *Woodward* and C. *Perrow* who analyzed the relationship between technology and organization structure, and P.R. *Lawrence* and J.W. *Lorsch* who considered the relationship between the task environment and organizational processes. Finally, there is the system approach which admits that the multiple fit between contingency factors and organizational variables leads to high performance. Organization design theorists such as J.D. *Thompson* and J.R. *Galbraith* take on this perspective. *Galbraith/Nathanson* (1978) indicate the multiple-level fit between organizational design variables, and maintain that the fit between strategy, structure and process brings out high performance as shown in Figure 1.

Thus, Contingency Theory consistently asserts the relationship between the fit and high performance. However, does the fit always assure high performance? According to *Thompson* (1967), technology and task environment are conflicting contingencies that have incompatible effects on organization. Actually, in multi-divisional organization, for instance, the upper level of organization deals with task environmental uncertainty (diversification of demand) through the product-oriented decision-making, while the lower level copes

Figure 1: Major Illustration on Fit Among an Organization's Design Variables

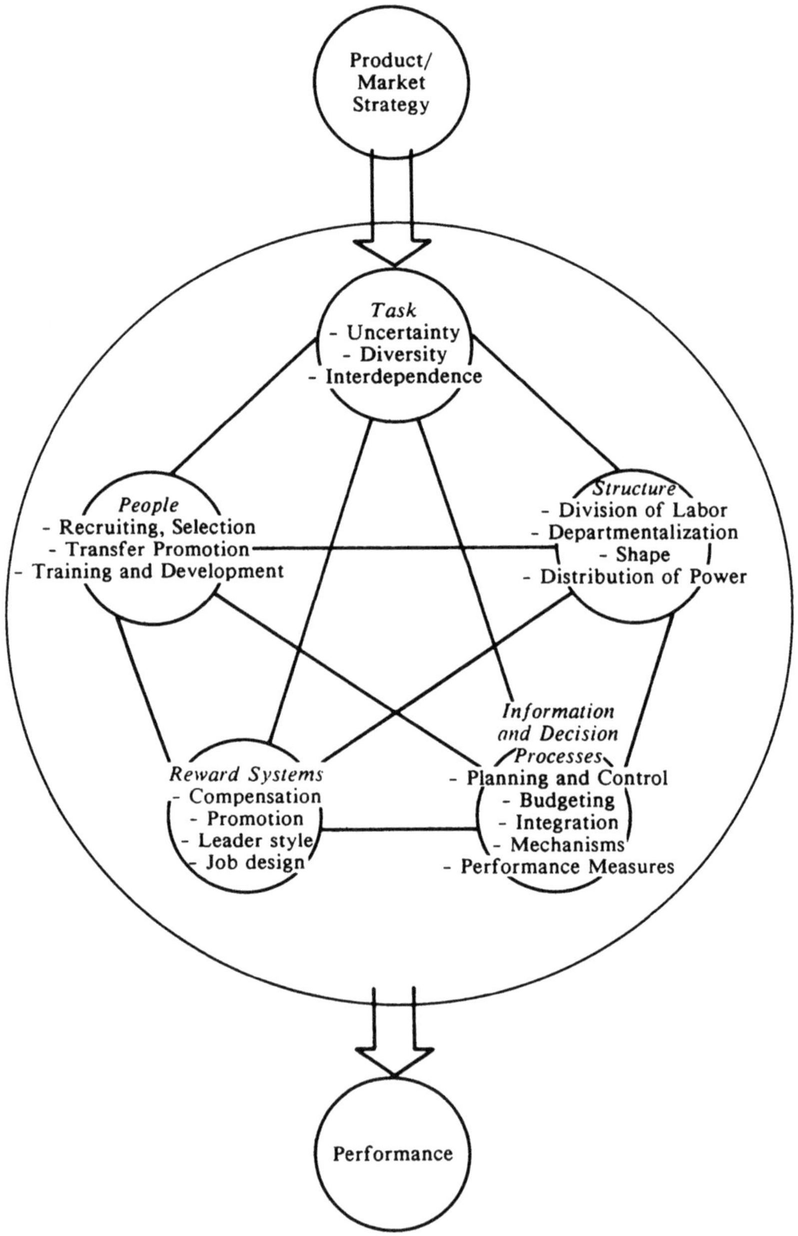

Source: *Galbraith/Nathanson* 1978.

with technological complexity (concentration of supply) through functional specialization. Moreover, it is generally said that divisionalized organization favors decentralization, and that functionalized organization prefers centralization. There are conflicting factors in organization, and it is the essence of management that coordinates those factors.

2. Ambivalence in organization

Davis/Lawrence (1977) state dilemmas in organization as follows. All forms of social organization have two simultaneous needs that are often at odds with each other: freedom and order. Freedom springs from intuition and leads to innovation. Order stems from intelligence and provides efficiency. Both are essential. Within organizations, freedom is interpreted as the specialized interest of different parts of an organization; the optimal goal of decentralization. Order is represented as the regulation and integration of all elements in harmonious and common action: the optimal goal of centralization. The problem with the centralization-decentralization debate, however, was that the more you realized the benefits of one, the less you obtained the benefits of the other. The dilemma of organization was the dilemma of an either-or world, of being either a boss or a subordinate. The promise of a release from the dilemma, is the flexibility of both centralization and decentralization, specialization and integration. The price, however, is real - it is a result of greater management and organizational complexity.

A more detailed analysis of Contingency Theory reveals the existence of conflicting factors and dilemmas in organization.

According to *Perrow* (1968), technology development is twofold. One is the case toward impersonal control in which a machine deals with complex problems and man confronts simple problems, as the technology develops. Another case is that of personal control in which complex problems are dealt with by man's problem-solving ability though machine treats only simple tasks. Thus, in non-routine technology with both characteristics of technology development, polycentralized organization structure is needed.

The key organizational strategy of *Lawrence/Lorsch* (1967) is differentiation and integration. High performing plastics organization, with high uncertainty in the task environment, introduced complex integrating mechanisms (e.g. integrator) in order to realize both high differentiation and high integration.

Thompson (1967) found the technology and the task environment as two significant and conflicting contingencies that gave organization uncertainty. It is necessary for organization to seal off the impact from the task environment in order to optimize technological rationality. Strategy of vertical integration and functionally departmentalized organization satisfy this demand well. However, when the task environment has high priority in decision-making, multi-divisional organization is appropriate under the diversification strategy. Furthermore, when we consider these two contingencies at the same time, it is necessary that task-force structure is overlaid by the functionally departmentalized organization for ordinary operations.

Weick (1979), who insists on the model opposite to that of Contingency Theory, also points out such conflicting factors in organization. Flexibility is needed for organization to cope with the environmental changes. However, it may deny repetitive past responses, and neglect identity and continuity. On the contrary, stability gives economic means to deal with unfamiliar contingencies, though it creates difficulty in finding environmental changes and more economic responses. These two contradicting processes are indispensable to organizational viability.

The same arguments are prevalent in the theory of innovation. The so-called "innovation dilemma" is such a case. *Duncan* (1976) explains the different effects of innovation on complexity, formalization, and centralization dimensions of organization structure. On the one hand, high complexity, low formalization, and decentralization are appropriate in the stage of initiation. On the other hand, low complexity, high formalization, and centralization are favorable in the stage of implementation.

Quin/Cameron (1988) point out that characteristics of effective organization are paradoxical.

1. Loose coupling and tight coupling: The former encourages wide search and initiation of innovation, and functional autonomy. The latter encourages quick execution, implementing innovation, and functional interdependence.

2. High specialization of roles and high generality of roles: The former serves expertise and efficiency. The latter serves flexibility and interdependence.

3. Continuity of leadership and infusion of new leaders: The former permits stability, long-term planning, and institutional memory. The latter permits increased innovation, adaptability, and currency.

4. Deviation-amplifying process and deviation-counteracting process: The former allows productive conflict and opposition that vitalize organization. The latter allows harmony and consensus needed to engender trust and smooth information flows.

5. Expanded search and creation of inhibitors to information overload: The former reinforces wider environmental scanning, access to more information, and divergence of input. The latter reinforces reduction in information flows reaching decision-makers, and convergence in decision-making.

6. Disengagement and disidentification with past strategies and reintegration and reinforcement of roots: The former fosters new perspectives and innovation and inhibits the tendency to define new problems simply as variations on old problems. The latter fosters commitment to a special sense of organizational identity and mission and past strategies.

In order to be successful, effective organization must manage these conflicting characteristics in organization simultaneously. A variety of contradictory factors in organization listed above is summarized in Table 1 along with the conservatism-liberalism dimension.

This organizational paradox results from the contradiction between the following two standards.

The first paradox is between "organizing" and "organized". This is explained as follows in Figure 2. It should interlock human behavior to form an organization. Each individual with self-interest would like to act for his own profit. However, when he cannot attain his goal by himself, he wants to exploit someone. Two individuals form an organization only when they realize each interest through mutual exploitation. Here organization is "consciously coordinated activities or forces by two or more persons" (*Barnard* 1938). Once for all be-

Table 1: Conservatism and Liberalism in Organization

Conservatism	liberalism
order	freedom
stability	flexibility
efficiency	effectiveness
specialization	problem-solving
functional management	general management
input control	output control
behavior control	result control
centralization	decentralization
mechanistic impersonal	organic personal
internal standard	external standard

Figure 2: Process of Organizational Development

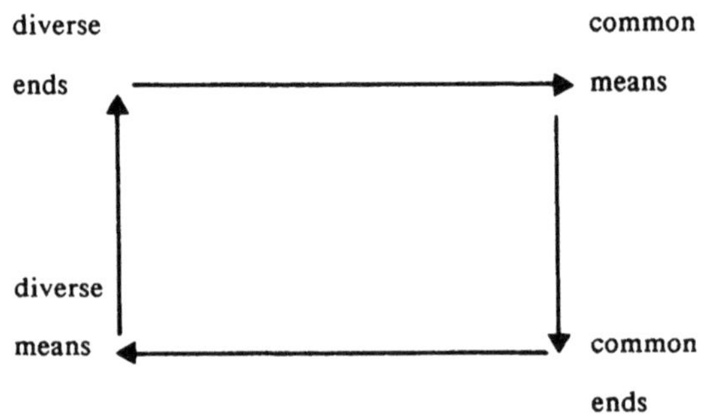

Source: *Weick* 1979.

havioral exposition can be called organization as far as it consists of interlocked behavior.

Next time when these two persons want to reach their own goals, (1) if the first interlocking gives an output better than his own aspiration level, (2) if he cannot find another partner who gives higher output, and (3) if interlocking of behavior with the first partner economizes the cost of search for another partner, they once again join their behavior. Thus, the fact that the same partner gives a certain level of satisfaction replaces the ends by the means. At first, organization was formed to attain his own individual goal, while now an individual goal is always attained only when he interlocks his behavior with the same partner. Here, transformation is performed from organization as means to organization as ends. In this sense, common ends become one of three requisites of organizational formation (*Barnard* 1938). In this case, common ends are literally the survival of once-formed organization, and continuous interlocking is considered to assure a mutual interest.

In this way, when organizational formation as such becomes self-purpose, division of labor arises in order to enable more efficient organizational survival. This means "diverse means", which contain two types. One is horizontal division of labor: research, production, and sales, etc. Another is vertical division of labor: strategic decision-making, administrative decision-making, and operational decision-making. Moreover, the realization of division of labor leads again to diverse ends.

In Figure 2, organization when formed as a common means is a process of interlocking behavior, and called loose coupling. In this sense, it can denote "organizing", by which organization as a result of interlocking behavior is meant. On the contrary, organization when formed as a diverse means refers to a departmentalized or divisionalized structure, which is called tight coupling-"organized". Organization in the former sense is rooted in an open & natural system model. Opposed to this, organization in the latter sense is based on an open & rational model. *Barnard* represents an intermediate position (closed & natural system model) between these two in the sense that he presupposes organization with a common purpose of organizational survival.

The second paradox is between "internal standard" and "external standard". Internal standard relates to stability. If each behavior contributes to mutual benefit, interlocked behavior is reinforced, and the trend toward internal stability is evoked without any relationship to the system adaptation to its environment. Therefore, internal standard as substitute for external standard is easy to be applicated. Namely, it functions well when the environment is certain and unchanged.

3. Paradox and organization design

What mechanisms does organization provide in order to manage such a paradox as described above?

On the individual level, a person decides for participation in an organization when incentives are larger than contributions. Each individual has a dual relationship to organization as individual personality and organizational personality. Organization has a pressure toward homogeneity and identification on the one hand. People love and interact with those who resemble themselves. On the other hand, however, it is not because agreement is gained but because profit is given that people have any interest for others. Consequently, organization put the individual in an ambivalent situation in identifying similarity for coherence (socialization) and in identifying heterogeneity for individuality (individuation).

On the departmental level, the following points are counted. For example, the production department has a dilemma in relation to initiation and implementation of innovation. In the initiation stage, the production group has an interest in new feasible products, and cooperates toward a new product idea. Thus, this group is decentralized. Whereas, in the implementation stage, close operational procedures are developed, and the production group is centralized. One of the important methods to treat this conflict is confrontation meeting; gate keeper, liaison role, and integrator coordinate this process. Another means to resolve conflict and disagreement in initiation and implementation is organizational development.

On the interdepartmental level, we can say the following. The prime interest of the production department are cost reductions, process efficiency, and technology improvement. Those of the sales department are customers, competitors, and other market factors. Those of the R & D department are development of scientific knowledge, applied new products, and development of new process technology.

Now, we compare the production department with the R & D department. The R & D department confronts an uncertain scientific subenvironment, and has characteristics of scientific goal orientation, longer time orientation, task orientation, low formality of structure, and decentralization. On the contrary, the production department deals with a certain techno-economic subenvironment, and is characterized as having low formality of structure, short-run time orientation, task orientation, and production cost and production technology orientation.

There is also a paradox in decision-making. *Petit* (1967) explains the difference between strategic decision-making and operational decision-making as follows. Strategic decision-making, from a long-run perspective, decides on a certain direction of the firm in order to deal with environmental uncertainty. Operational decision-making, based on short-run perspective, copes with a quantifiable repetitive problem.

As described above, organization design is a resolution to conflicting demands in organization. It is strategy that gives priority to certain conflicting factors.

Under the strategy of vertical integration, functional decision-making has a priority, and is adopted to functionally departmentalized organization, in which functional decision-making is performed at the higher level of hierarchy. The strategy of product diversification deserves high priority in product-oriented decision-making, which is treated at the upper level of hierarchy. Therefore, this strategy favors multi-divisional organization. Functionally departmentalized organization is centralized in the sense that general management is concentrated on the top level of management; yet multi-divisional organization is decentralized, because part of general management is delegated to the lower level of organization. When we give the same priority to the two factors, or need a quick change in strategy, matrix organization is introduced. This is a resolution to simultaneously cope with the conflicting needs of concentration of supply and diversification of demand at the same level. Here, general management is delegated to a much lower level (decentralization), and at the same time, is necessary performance orientation of organization as a whole (centralization). Moreover, matrix organization is a form that built in high differentiation and high integration at the same time. This is an effort to introduce flexibility in stability of structure.

4. Paradox and organizational change

4.1. Framework

Van de Ven/Poole (1988) show that we must resolve the following 4 paradoxes in order to understand organizational transformation.

1. Behavior-structure paradox: we must explain both individual motivation (part) and collective structure (whole), and make clear the relationship between behavior and structure.

2. Internal factors-external factors paradox: we must describe organizational transformation for both internal and external factors.

3. Stability-instability paradox: we must analyze both stability (uniformity, consensus, and order) and change (conflict, pluralism, and disruption).

4. We need an explanation from historical and diachronic perspective.

We have four methods to solve these paradoxes.

1. Comparative analysis: a method to enumerate conflicting hypotheses, and to evaluate each form of organizational problem-solving.

2. Relational analysis: a method to identify to which level each of the conflicting hypotheses refers, and specify the relationship between these hypotheses.

3. Dynamic analysis: a method to explain the relationship between structure and behavior historically.

4. Conceptual analysis: a method to develop new concepts showing the relationship between structure and behavior.

Below, we depict how these four methods of analysis are applied to the three paradoxes mentioned above.

4.2. Behavior-structure paradox

Behavior is guided by structure, but structure is formed only by behavior. Action theory emphasizes the former position by asserting that frequent interaction of individual behavior results in the formation of structure. Structuralists agree with the latter perspective, contending that structure is a source of behavioral patterns.

a) Comparative analysis

Paradoxes on each level of inquiry are as follows: (1) individual level - the problem of selecting, socializing, and controlling individuals according to roles and positions vs. the problem of how human behavior reformulates these roles and positions. (2) Departmental level - the problem is whether or not the departmental structure affects the socio-psychological characteristics (collective norms, interaction pattern, conflict, and power relationship). (3) Organizational level - the problem is whether or not the organization structure influences environmental change and strategic choice. (4) Interorganizational level - the problem is whether or not the organizational domain or the market structure is limited by various forms of political bargaining.

The above contradiction presents a paradox between the rational model and the natural system model. Contingency Theory, which is based on the open & rational model, presupposes that the causal relationship is between environment → organization → human. In contrast, Theory of Organizing, which is based on the open & natural system model, premises that the causal relationship is between human → organization → environment. The organizational model of Barnard is based on the closed & natural system model in which the causal relationship of environment → organization ← human is presupposed and here the common goal is given. The open & rational model dictates an organization design in which the organization is arranged according to its environment. However, in the open & natural system model, environmental manipulation is implemented in order for organization to change its environment. The final stage of environmental manipulation is the strategic maneuvering to absorb the environmental uncertainty. According to this final strategy, administrative problems arise and organization stucture is reformed. This is the very situation where *Chandler* (1962) says that structure follows strategy.

b) Relational analysis

This analysis should provide both (a) a series of hypotheses of how individual interests and goals relate to one another through the action system and (b) a series of relational rules for integrating individual actions into collective acts (*Coleman* 1986). We have three types of action systems: market, hierarchy, and federation. A market consists of independent actors with different interests and goals. A federation is composed of independent actors with common interests. Hierarchy brings about an authority relationship to coordinate members' interests as an organization. These three are a means of coordinating interorganizational relationship.

c) Dynamic analysis

The influences of structure and behavior are bilateral, but the strength is dependent on the phases over time. In the first phase, the existing structure regulates behavior. In the second phase, behavior evokes the attention to the alternative structure. In the third phase, new structure is reformed and institutionalized.

Tushman/Romanelli (1985), in their model of punctuated equilibrium, distinguished the phase of convergence and that of reorientation. The former is a stage of hightening the degree of congruence among structure, system, control and resource. The latter refers to a period of discontinuous change in which strategies, power, structure, and systems are fundamentally transformed toward a new basis of alignment.

The transformation from one congruence to another means the total change in all the variables of organizational structure, that is structural reformation. A congruence forms a configuration (Gestalt). On the way of reformation, it is behavior or process, not structure, which changes. Structure is a stable and economic means to cope with environmental change. It is behavior that deals with new and intermittent changes in the environment. When new problems are so frequent and important that organization has to manage them at the top of the hierarchy, strategic change is needed and finally structural reformation is revived.

d) Conceptual analysis

For example, *Giddens'* (1985) structuration parallels this method. Structuration is the process of production and reproduction of social systems via members' application of rules and resources. Structure refers to the rules and resources to be applied in interaction. A system is a result of this application of rules and resources, and the observable patterns of relationship between people and groups. Therefore, structure has dual roles that lead action as well as is produced and reproduced through the interaction between people.

4.3. Internal-external paradox

Developmentalism argues that change is set in motion from within the organization, while accumulation theories posit that change comes from outside the organization. In the former, change is immanent and continuous. Namely, organization has its logic, programs, and codes that regulate change process, and can gain some dictated outcome from the start, when given the initial conditions. Moreover, organization changes gradually like a selection process in the theory of natural selection. Accumulation theories of social change emphasize that growth of organization or new organizational development is performed through the external conditions of environmental change or human interference.

a) Comparative analysis

Here the essential contradiction is between environmental determinism and strategic choice. Contingency Theory, the natural selection model, and the structural-functional analysis are representatives of the former view. The latter perspective contains the strategic choice model and collective action theory. Environmental determinism posits that change is immanent and continuous, and that structural differentiation, integration, and adaptation proceed gradually. The strategic choice model stresses that purposeful individuals select and form the social institution.

The following caution must be taken. Contingency Theory is environmental determinism in that it asserts organizations with high performance fit to their environment. However, it is based on the rational model which presumed the rational choice of the top management, while the natural selection model and structural-functionalism are rooted in the natural system model. Consequently, organizational development in Contingency Theory is to be a stage-wise development accompanied by structual (Gestalt) change.

b) Relational analysis

Accumulation theories refer to a discrete and incontinuous process of reorientation, while the developmental model is applied in the period of continuous convergence in the punctuated equilibrium model (*Tushman/Romanelli* 1985).

c) Dynamic analysis

The natural selection model and collective action theory are macro-scopic, whereas Contingency Theory and the strategic choice model are micro-scopic. When individuals behave independently, it is exogeneous to structure, yet when individuals have roles or positions in an organization it is endogeneous. At the different level of analysis, both developmental change and accumulative change are observable on the macro and micro levels at the same time. Therefore, the degree of coupling and interdependence is more important than endogeneity or exogeneity of change.

d) Conceptual analysis

Sztompka (1979) distinguishes the individual as an active subject from that as a passive object. This shows the degree to which an individual can control his behavior. The individual as an active subject has the power to control his own situation, and to plan and decide to select his action course. The individual as a passive subject subjugates to pressures and has no power to control.

Contingency Theory presupposes the rational manager in the sense that *Hazewinkel* (1984) ironically defines the concept of "fit". Namely, the fit between structure and organizational environment means that the structure is the most efficient under the given goal and the existing knowledge of the situation. On the contrary, the strategic choice model considers the manager who prefers the fit or congruency among organizational design variables. A manager makes organizational design to fit the strategy he selects for himself.

4.4. Stability-instability paradox

a) Comparative analysis

Stability and instability appear according to the difference of the level of analysis. Contingency Theory explains the stable fit between organization and environment. Individuals who make a strategic choice act for their own political interest within this system equilibrium of fit which Contingency Theory dictates.

b) Relational analysis

Hernes (1976) admits three structural dimensions of organizational change. The first is the output structure which denotes the allocation of the result. The second is the process structure to specify the logical types of process leading to the result. The third is the parameter structure to regulate this process. Stability and instability is a result of forces (collective behavior and environment) to work on the structure which maintains and changes parameter, process, and output. First is the simple reproduction which means stability. Second is the expanded reproduction which is the case of change in output. Third is the transition of change in parameter and output. Fourth is the transformation to mean the change in process, parameter, and output.

c) Dynamic analysis

According to *Hernes* (1976), the first stage is that action is regulated by the existing structure. In the second stage, actors try to innovate and adapt through the institution. Here, the forces to regulate the individuals' adaptability to the institutional structure are important. Stability and instability depend on the degree of individuals' discretion. In the third stage, the system is reproduced.

d) Conceptual analysis

The theory of structuration implies that action in the organization is continuously producing and reproducing the process and output structures. Therefore, a model must show how particular structural features enter into action and thereby maintain and change the process and parameter structures. Because action is context-bound, this model must allow for different outcomes, depending on the particular actors involved, the context, and how action unfolds.

An individual forms his reality socially. He sees reality based on his own image, and behaves according to that image. He views his behavior in retrospect and makes sense of it. This is the "enacted environment". There is no objective stability and instability. It changes according to the sense-making behavior of people.

5. Concluding remarks

This article pointed out the existence of the paradox inherent in organization, and based on this perspective, reviewed the characteristics of the Contingency Theory which insisted on the fit or congruency consistently. Organization design is a coordination of this paradox. There are four methods to solve this paradox, according to which three kinds of paradoxes are analyzed.

It is, as such, an innovation to cope with paradox. However, organization causes pressure toward the selection of internal standard and stability.

Child, *Ganter* and *Kieser* (1987) identify eight sources of organizational conservatism.

1. Organization inclines to introduce new equipment compatible with existing organization structure.

2. Innovative changes in investment and the organization design are so costly and interdependent that the organizational status quo is a powerful consideration.

3. A person in the power position wants to redesign so as to stabilize his position, and to increase his influences.

4. Organization philosophy and principles with long history in organization have a large impact on the way of perceiving organization problems and their solution.

5. If cost-benefit analyses are required, more radical designs are ruled out because those analyses are difficult to estimate.

6. Organizational principles and rules of good practices are embedded within the culture of a society. Organizations that violate these principles by being innovative run the risk of loosing legitimacy.

7. Existing qualifications and legal regulation often excludes such a redesign as it would require new qualifications and jobs.

8. Participation is usually seen as a means of overcoming resistance to change. However, it diminishes the likelihood that radical organizational solutions will be accepted, because a workers' council may reject the introduction of new technologies in order to defend existing employment levels and qualification structures.

Random variation is often said to be a means of overcoming the resistance to change. However, this is not always so, since randomness increases entropy according to the second law of thermodynamics. In order to bring about self-organization, there must be some rule necessary for the evolution before the selection of the specific factors. What are the rules that regulate the evolution in organization? In organization design, the technology and the task environment are the two essential dimensions, and according to these two dimensions conflicting factors such as centralization and decentralization, specialization and order, and stability and flexibility etc. are put in order. Organization design is a kind of readjustment of conflicting factors in such a way that a group of factors is dealt with at a higher level of hierarchy, and another group of factors at a lower level. Therefore, organization design which takes these dimensions into account is more likely to lead self-organization than random variation.

References

Barnard, C. I., The Functions of the Executive, Cambridge, Mass. (Harvard University Press) 1938

Chandler, A. D., Strategy and Structure, Cambridge, Mass. (MIT Press) 1962

Child, J., Organizational Design and Performance: Contingency Theory and Beyond, Organization and Administrative Sciences, Vol. 2 & 3, 1977

Coleman, J. S., Social Theory, Social Research, and a Theory of Action, American Journal of Sociology, Vol. 16, 1986

Davis, S. M./*Lawrence*, P. R., Matrix, Reading, Mass. (Addison-Wesley) 1977

Duncan, R. B., The Ambidextrous Organization: Designing Dual Structures for Innovations, in: R. H. *Kilman*/L. R. *Pondy*/D. P. *Slevin* (eds.), The Management of Organization Design, Vol. 1, New York (North-Holland) 1976

Galbraith, J. R./*Nathanson*, D. A., Strategy Implementation: The Role of Structure and Process, St. Paul, Minnesota (West Publishing) 1978

Ganter, H.-D./*Kieser*, A., Technological Innovation and Organizational Concervatism, in: J. M. *Pennings*/A. *Buitendam* (eds.), New Technology as Organizational Innovation, Cambridge, Mass. (Ballinger) 1987

Giddens, A., The Construction of Society, (University of California Press) 1985

Hazewinkel, A., Organization Structure and Contingency Theory, in: P. J. *Drenth*/ H. *Thierry*/P. J. *Wilemms*/C. J. *de Wolff* (eds.), Handbook of Work and Organizational Psychology, New York (John Wiley & Sons) 1984

Hernes, G., Structural Change in Social Processes, American Journal of Sociology, Vol. 82, No. 3, 1976

Perrow, C., The Effect of Technological Change on the Structure of Business Firm, in: B. C. *Roberts* (ed.), Industrial Relations: Contemporary Issues, New York (Macmillan) 1968

Petit, T. A., A Behavioral Theory of Management, Academy of Management Journal, Vol. 10, No. 4, 1967

Sztompka, P., Sociological Dilemmas: Towards a Dialectical Paradigm, New York (Free Press) 1979

Thompson, J. D., Organizations in Action, New York (McGraw-Hill) 1967

Tushman, M. L. and *Romanelli*, E., Organizational Evolution: A Metamorphosis Model of Convergence and Reorientation, in: B. M. *Staw*/L. L. *Cummings* (eds.), Research in Organizational Behavior, Vol. 7, Greenwich, Conneticut (JAI Press) 1985

Van de Ven, A. H./*Poole*, M. S., Paradoxical Requirements for a Theory of Organizational Change, in: R. E. *Quinn*/K. S. *Cameron* (eds.), Paradox and Transformation: Towards a Theory of Change in Organization and Management, Cambridge, Mass. (Ballinger) 1988

Weick, K. E., The Social Psychology of Organizing, 2nd ed., Reading, Mass. (Addison-Wesley) 1979

Contributors

ARAYAMA Yuko is associate professor of agricultural policy in the Faculty of Economics of Nagoya University

Theodor DAMS is emeritus professor of economic policy in the Faculty of Economics of Freiburg University

Wolfgang HILKE is professor of business administration in the Faculty of Economics of Freiburg University

ITOH Masanao is associate professor of Japanese economic history in the Faculty of Economics of Nagoya University

KANEGAE Tsuyoshi is associate professor of public finance in the Faculty of Economics of Chukyo University

KISHIDA Tamiki is associate professor of business administration in the Faculty of Economics of Nagoya University

Oliver LANDMANN is professor of economics in the Faculty of Economics of Freiburg University

MATSUGI Takashi is professor of agricultural policy in the Faculty of Economics of Nagoya University

Alois OBERHAUSER is professor of public finance in the Faculty of Economics of Freiburg University

OGAWA Eiji is professor of business administration in the Faculty of Economics of Nagoya University

OKUMURA Ryuhei is associate professor of international economics in the Faculty of Economics of Nagoya University

Bernd ROHWER is lecturer (Privatdozent) in the Faculty of Economics of Freiburg University and head of the planning staff in the Prime Minister's Office of Schleswig-Holstein (Germany)

Ralf-Bodo SCHMIDT is professor of business administration in the Faculty of Economics of Freiburg University

MIX
Papier aus verantwortungsvollen Quellen
Paper from responsible sources
FSC® C105338

Printed by Libri Plureos GmbH
in Hamburg, Germany